BEYOND PROMISES

Ron Corbett

With Rick Smith

Big Fox Publishing

ISBN-13: 978-1544627694
ISBN: 1544627696

Library of Congress Control Number: 2017936681

©2017 Ron Corbett
Printed in the U.S.A.

Big Fox Publishing
75 Commercial Drive, #170
P. O. Box 170
North Liberty, IA 52317
www.bigfoxpublishing.com

To my exceptional sisters—
for their strength and perseverance

CONTENTS

PROLOGUE

TAKING ACCOUNT

I entered public life 30 years ago, when I took the oath of office and a seat in the Iowa House of Representatives.

I've been in the public eye most of the time since: Thirteen years as a Republican in the Iowa House, five of those as House speaker; six years at the Cedar Rapids Area Chamber of Commerce as president and chief executive officer; and now into my eighth year as mayor of Cedar Rapids.

This book is a memoir of sorts about those times and others. It's written through my eyes. I do nearly all the talking.

These chapters aren't filled with adulation from friends and hand-picked colleagues. Nor do I take time to ask the opinions of others, including those who have disagreed with me over the years.

It's a given: Others surely have a different version of me than I do.

If there are mistakes in the book, they are mine.

It might be considered audacious to write about yourself and your travels. But I wanted to. I wanted to take stock of where I've been, what I've done, and, maybe, who I am.

I'm a Christian, for one. I'm a father, an American, an Iowan.

My faith is important to me. I carry it with me. Still, I know I'm not a pastor; politicians have a different calling. But elected officials can learn plenty from pastors—like the ability to listen and to show compassion.

I'm writing this book, too, at a remarkable moment for Cedar Rapids as we have picked ourselves up from a historic flood disaster in 2008.

I hope the book serves to chronicle that comeback.

My youngest son, Thomas, asked me recently if a community reflects its leader or the leader reflects the community. What a thought from a high school junior. Maybe it's both, I told him.

With the arrival of 2017 has come speculation about who will run for Iowa governor in 2018 now that the state's long-serving governor, Terry Branstad, is stepping down to become the United States ambassador to China.

People have suggested I might. But as I finish writing this in early 2017, I don't know yet.

What I do know is this: Serving in elective office is like coming back from a long missionary trip to the other side of the world. You always feel like you've gotten more than you gave.

I long have started each day thinking things can get better. Here in Cedar Rapids and Iowa and beyond. I still think that. I can' t imagine it any differently. The comfortable and customary can be right for many things. But not for everything.

I

STRENGTHENED BY HIGH WATER

Somewhere south of Mason City, the clouds opened and a deluge of rain pounded down, sending cars creeping to the highway's shoulder to wait out the worst of it.

My friend and associate, Andy Anderson, was behind the wheel, pushing on. In the back seat, I was reading mayoral emails and preparing a speech to give to a Rotary Club the next morning on water quality and modernizing Iowa's income tax code.

Our windshield wipers couldn't keep up. Sixty-five miles an hour had slowed to 15.

I was aware that it had been an odd September 2016, with weeks of late summer storms north of Cedar Rapids in the Cedar River watershed. I knew, too, that protracted heavy rain up there can mean flooding downstream in Cedar Rapids. But this was September. It never floods in September in Iowa.

Even so, I texted our city manager, Jeff Pomeranz, to tell him about the rain around Mason City and to find out if the Cedar River was behaving in Cedar Rapids. It was.

But the rain up north fell all night, pelting the windows and rattling in the motel gutters and downspouts. I hardly slept a minute.

At my 7 a.m. speaking event, all anyone could talk about was the 10 inches of rain the night before. I did a brief TV news interview after the speech, but the newsroom was abuzz about rain, not about my messages on water quality and income taxes.

Pomeranz phoned me. The National Weather Service now was predicting that the Cedar River at Cedar Rapids would rise within days to near historic levels. I canceled the rest of my schedule and hurried home.

As I pulled into Cedar Rapids, the river-level prediction had jumped to 24 feet, 4 feet higher than at any time in more than 160 years of Cedar Rapids history—not counting the city's flood disaster of June 2008 when the river reached 31.12 feet.

I had spent seven years as mayor helping to lead Cedar Rapids through the recovery from one devastating flood, and now we were facing the prospect of another. Much of our rebuilding after 2008 suddenly stood in harm's way.

It made me think about the movie "Apollo 13." There's that scene when the NASA flight director dumps a box of odds and ends and spare parts on a desk and tells the engineers to figure out a way to get the disabled Apollo spacecraft and astronaut Jim Lovell—played by Tom Hanks—and his crew home.

It felt just like that when I spoke at a news conference at City Hall to promise residents that we would find a way to protect Cedar Rapids from what looked like 2008 all over again.

I intended it to be more than a promise.

As the river rose, city crews, with the help of private contractors, erected 9.8 miles of HESCO barriers—big, wire-mesh baskets that are filled with sand—and dirt berms in a couple of days. Musco Lighting of Oskaloosa, Iowa, provided lighting so the work could continue through the night, and the University of Iowa sold us some of its HESCOs to bolster our supply.

We designed the emergency plan to protect the city to a flood crest of 26 feet. A cadre of mostly citizen volunteers filled another 250,000 sandbags and placed them around businesses and homes as a second line of defense. As a final defense, we asked some 8,000 people to evacuate homes and businesses at risk of flooding.

"If it works, we will have saved the city," I said at the news conference on Sept. 26, the day before the flood crest.

Then we waited and watched as the river made its final climb and rising water began to threaten some of the HESCOs and berms. In places, water seeped through the barriers, and in other spots, water came up from the storm sewers.

"We built a temporary system. It's not safe. It's not permanent," Jen Winter, the city's public works director, warned when many in the at-risk area had not left.

I said any sightseer on foot or on a bicycle near the berms and HESCOs didn't stand a chance in the event of a breach.

But there weren't any. The makeshift flood protection held. We had averted a second flood disaster in eight years. In the end, the river got to 21.95 feet on Tuesday, Sept. 27—the second-highest crest in city history—before receding.

Holding back the high water of September 2016 in Cedar Rapids captured plenty of national news attention because the city had survived a devastating flood so recently. As mayor, I was asked dozens of times how the city had been able to protect itself this time. I said it wasn't just that Cedar Rapids residents and Iowans are good people. Good people are other places, too.

No, we beat back the flood because we hadn't forgotten the scars and memories of 2008. We still remembered the ruined, water-soaked photos, clothes, furniture and every other kind of possession stacked outside homes. We still felt the claws of heavy equipment grabbing it all up and dropping it into dump trucks on the way to the landfill.

I think, too, that Cedar Rapids had come a long way since 2008, and residents knew that. We had gained a new-found strength in disaster and the recovery from it. We felt a sense of achievement. We didn't want to lose that. We didn't want to see it ruined.

The year 2008 had been unbelievable. That June, things fell apart when a downpour hit as the flooding river was cresting—a worst-case nightmare that sent water over 10 square miles of the city, covering 1,126 city blocks.

Of those, 561 blocks took a major hit. The water entered 6,865 residential properties, forced more than 10,000 residents out of their homes and affected 754 commercial and industrial properties, including much of the downtown. All the city's major public buildings were damaged or ruined.

There was City Hall, sticking out of the river from its flooded home on May's Island. Tanker cars and the train bridge beneath them had toppled into the floodwater next to downtown. Harbor houses ripped from their moorings were stacked downstream, one on top of another.

By 2016, I was finishing my seventh year as mayor, and

I had grown accustomed to reciting a long list of victories to document the quality of the city's recovery and its transformation after the 2008 disaster.

With a mix of private investment and public disaster grants, 866 new replacement homes and about 2,000 apartment and condominium units were built in the city, many in flood-impacted older neighborhoods but out of harm's way. Also, more than 2,300 flood-damaged homes and apartment units were renovated.

Today, too, there is a new greenway stretching along the river where some 1,300 flood-ruined homes once stood and have been demolished.

The city has a new downtown library, central fire station, convention center, public works building, animal control facility and federal courthouse. City Hall (now in the former federal courthouse), the Paramount Theatre, the Veterans Memorial Building and the bus depot all have been renovated.

In addition, the city purchased the downtown's lone hotel out of bankruptcy and brought it back to life. Two flooded commercial and residential districts, New Bohemia and Kingston Village, now are full of life and growing next to downtown, which itself has welcomed a post-flood burst in building and housing. Also, across the river from downtown is the new riverfront amphitheater, which ingeniously doubles as a piece of the city's coming flood protection system.

One thing about disasters: News reporters and cameras move on, and recovery and rebuilding take over.

And they take time: Years and years, day by day, out of the limelight.

In my annual State of the City Address in 2017, I told a short story I borrowed from a friend. In it, a man comes upon two stone cutters, both hard at work. One is cussing and swearing and the other has little to say. Each is asked what he is doing, and the first says he is doing what it looks like, cutting a stone. The second, disinterestedly, says he is cutting a stone for some sort of building.

Then the man approaches a third stone cutter who is smiling and whistling as he works. He sets aside his hammer and chisel when asked what he is doing, and, beaming, he proclaims, "I am building a cathedral."

That is how I have felt as Cedar Rapids' mayor, helping to direct the city's recovery from the disaster that hit in 2008.

We never lost sight of the big picture—that we were rebuilding a city better than it ever had been, as if it were a cathedral. It is a remarkable story of partnership between the public and the private sectors and of a promise fulfilled.

As 2017 begins, Cedar Rapids is 1-1 with the river in eight years. We've evened the score.

Without a permanent flood protection system in place, though, a rematch very well may be in the offing. Who knows when. It may be this year, eight years from now, or years after that.

But we, as Cedar Rapids' city leaders, have promised that permanent flood protection is coming. And we're determined to make it more than a promise.

The protection system is being built now, piece by piece, year by year. It is work with a measure of hope: hope that funding for the protection's completion beats the next disaster to town.

2

DON'T JUST HOLD OFFICE

A piece of dinner napkin has taken its place in the clutter of keepsakes at Cedar Rapids City Hall.

On that napkin back in the fall of 2010, I sketched out a way for Cedar Rapids to secure state funds to protect itself from a repeat of its devastating 2008 flood.

City Manager Jeff Pomeranz saved the evidence, not me.

As he tells me, it is an important reminder of how the Iowa Flood Mitigation Board was created in 2012 and how it went on to award a total of $596.8 million to Cedar Rapids and nine other Iowa communities to help them build flood protection.

I suppose the remnant from a steak dinner is proof that ideas come from somewhere and from someone. Often it is a napkin, an outline on a scrap of paper or even a note to yourself on a smartphone that ends up being the only thing to memorialize the moment.

The thing with ideas is that beginnings can get murky. Competing authors can emerge. Ideas can be joint ventures, hatched amid brainstorms with others. And some ideas can be borrowed from earlier ones. My idea for the state's help on flood protection, for instance, shared some similarity to the way the state sales tax helped pay for construction of the Iowa Speedway in Newton, Iowa, in 2006.

But there are new things under the sun, too.

If one thing is true about me, it is that I don't like to sit around. Almost by necessity, ideas pop into my head, in part, because I'm not sure when other people will show up with their ideas. I get fidgety.

I did not become a state lawmaker, the head of the Cedar Rapids Area Chamber of Commerce or Cedar Rapids mayor just to hold the position. I didn't long to be an empty suit.

I've wanted to do things. I've liked trying out ideas, mine or someone else's, to see what might become of them—to see if life in Cedar Rapids and in Iowa ends up a little better.

Christopher Rants of Sioux City, who was among our group of young Republicans in the Iowa House of Representatives in the late 1990s, reminded me of the time I floated my version of the idea to create a Rebuild Iowa Infrastructure Fund or RIIF during an evening playing laser tag.

My infrastructure concept—there were other versions along the way—called for steering part of the growth in the state's annual take from gambling proceeds into the RIIF. That way, state funds would be available for needed building projects without having to take on debt.

Money from RIIF, which remains in place today, renovated the State Capitol, built a new Iowa Supreme Court building, updated Iowa State Fair facilities and paid for a new residential cottage at the State Training School for Boys in Eldora. The cottage is named Corbett-Miller Hall to acknowledge the effort Attorney General Tom

Miller and I made to support the project.

Rants also has told me that he and others in the House leadership used to wait every Monday morning to see what new ideas I had concocted over the weekend. They weren't all winners. Some of those great ideas went right into the trash can, Brent Siegrist of Council Bluffs, another of those Republican House leaders, is still quick to remind me.

One that didn't get thrown away was my idea for a special Iowa license plate that directed a fee per plate to the state's Resource Enhancement and Protection, or REAP, fund. My drawings for the plates, which are now called natural resources license plates, didn't excite anyone. I'm no artist. But the idea for the license plates did.

In my time in the Legislature, we also had diaper changing stations installed in a House chamber restroom, worked up the concept for planting a million trees in Iowa in a decade and crafted a proposal that led to the state's Community Attraction and Tourism, or CAT, grants. To date, those grants have provided $159 million in state funds to 427 community projects in 97 of Iowa's 99 counties in fewer than 20 years.

I didn't need a Legislature to launch an idea.

Amy Johnson, who was marketing and communications director during my time at the Chamber, still remembers the call I made to her from France in 2004 to mobilize what I called the Fifteen in 5 campaign. The idea was to identify and complete 15 community projects in five years.

"What's that noise?" Johnson remembers asking. "Are those horses?"

My wife at the time, who is from France, and I were staying at a bed-and-breakfast with a bedroom over a stable. Neighing horses were making a racket, and there was an aroma of hay in the room. But I still got my Fifteen in 5 plan through to Johnson.

Also in 2004, I began a petition drive through the Chamber with plenty of community support to change Cedar Rapids' old-fashioned city government into one with a professional city manager and a larger, more diverse, part-time City Council.

By June 2005, voters overwhelmingly approved the change, and in 2006, a new part-time mayor, part-time council and Cedar Rapids' first city manager moved in at City Hall.

So, some ideas do take flight—RIIF, the REAP license plates, the CAT grants, Fifteen in 5 and the new Cedar Rapids city government.

My idea of how to get state help for Cedar Rapids flood protection also came with its own moniker—GRI for Growth Reinvestment Initiative—provided by the napkin-saving city manager, Pomeranz.

That night in 2010 at dinner with Pomeranz, I drew out how Cedar Rapids and other Iowa communities could make a case to keep a share of the increase in state sales tax collected in a city for up to 20 years. That money would be used to help pay part of the cost of flood protection.

My thought was that a city's ability to grow and prosper, which Cedar Rapids has been able to do since its 2008 flood, increases state revenue from sales in the city. Why not reward cities and let them keep a piece of the tax growth to provide flood protection? After all, without the protection, the local economy might not be able to grow. In that case, the state also would lose tax revenue.

In 2015, I began to focus on how statewide issues such as water quality and storm runoff affect a city's drinking water and a city's ability to protect itself from flooding.

I've come to see, too, how a city like Cedar Rapids works long and hard to attract and keep businesses even as the state's outdated, uncompetitive income-tax system can drive potential employers and workers away.

With the idea that city issues are state ones and state issues are city ones, I've founded and operate a think tank, something of a conservative idea factory, as I continue to work as Cedar Rapids' part-time mayor.

I've named the new organization Engage Iowa.

3

ON THE ROAD TO ENGAGE IOWA

I probably never came all the way back from my days in the Iowa Statehouse.

In 1999, I left there by choice after 13 years, the last five as House speaker, so I could be home in Cedar Rapids full time with my family. My fifth child was due that September.

As I departed the Statehouse, my colleagues as well as statewide opinion-makers said things you can hang onto for a lifetime.

"Ron was the strongest adversary I've faced," Democratic House Minority Leader Dave Schrader of Monroe, Iowa, said at the time. "The Republican team just lost their (baseball star) Mark McGwire. Those sluggers don't come around that often."

Chuck Gipp, a House Republican from Decorah, used a sports analogy, too. "Anybody that fills the speaker's position will understand how Kirk Ferentz feels replacing Hayden Fry," he said.

David Yepsen, statewide political columnist for The Des Moines Register at the time, said my departure might appear to end the political ambitions of "a rising Republican star." But he doubted it. "He just may be too well-regarded by a lot of important people to remain out of politics forever," Yepsen said.

First-year Gov. Tom Vilsack, a Democrat, seemed to understand the pull to make more time for family.

"The legislative process will miss Speaker Corbett," Vilsack said. "It is a tremendous challenge to raise children in the public eye, particularly young children. ... You can always run for political office, whether you're 38 or 48 or 58. But you can only watch your children grow up once."

When I walked away, it wasn't because I was burned out. No. I left something I really wanted to do. I just had more important priorities in my life.

But my passion for public policy never died.

I still believe Iowa can be better. Public service doesn't mean just making sure meetings adjourn on time or getting buses to run on schedule. We can do more than keep things the same as usual.

This drive in me stretches back to my first run for elective office in 1986 at age 26.

I'm older now, and, I think, smarter, better informed, more well-rounded.

In 2010, I took over as Cedar Rapids' part-time mayor while holding down a job at trucking firm CRST, first as vice president of human resources and then as special projects manager.

Part time, I quickly learned, was something of a misnomer in a city that needed to recover and rebuild after the largest disaster in Iowa's history.

Today, though, Cedar Rapids is back on its feet, and I've been on the road part of each month with a new endeavor—a statewide policy think tank with a conservative bent that I call Engage Iowa.

My intent is for the think tank to provide the type of in-state expertise that I needed 20 years ago when I proposed a 15 percent cut in state income taxes while in the Iowa Legislature. Back then, I had to reach out to Boston, Mass., to find a credible conservative analyst to talk about taxation. Engage Iowa now can offer an analysis of Iowa issues from Iowa.

At Engage Iowa, I'm raising money to fund the enterprise, identifying experts to research and write issue papers and traveling across the state to discuss ideas and policy suggestions.

The travel is giving me a chance to take the temperature on topics for which consensus is always hard to find. Along the way, I'm learning what might and might not gain a following. And I'm seeing what might have enough support to make its way into policy debates at the Statehouse and governor's office in Des Moines.

By early 2017, I had spoken to Rotary Clubs and an assortment of other organizations in more than 60 of Iowa's 99 counties, big and small, urban and rural.

I'm a Rotarian, and Rotary Clubs have been a good place to be. Many Iowa towns have them, and most meet weekly. They need speakers, and I have something to speak about.

Water quality, water runoff, sales tax, income taxes, education. I'm not out there talking about the easy sells.

Thirty years ago, when I first entered the Iowa Legislature, Iowa was widely seen as leading the nation in education. But we have slipped.

I think it's time to look at bold ideas in education and not just be content to fight over incremental increases or decreases in annual state funding for schools.

Should Iowa, for instance, bolster the teaching profession? Should we reward our best teachers? Should our best take their skills to the virtual classroom so students across the state can benefit? How about more summer school classes so students don't regress between school years? Should districts limit what they spend on administration to 10 percent of their budgets?

On the economic front, Iowa in 2017 will celebrate the 20-year anniversary of its last major income-tax cut, a 10 percent, across-the-board reduction that I helped design and shepherd through the Iowa Legislature.

I'd like to take a fresh look at Iowa's income-tax structure, which I believe needs to be modernized, simplified and made more competitive with other states. The current set-up—with an 8.98 percent top income-tax rate that is fourth-highest among states—scares employers, new workers and retirees away from Iowa. It is a system, too, in which middle-income workers can pay at a higher tax rate than wealthier Iowans because of the morass of special deductions and tax credits that clutter the tax code.

The time also has come for Iowans to address the quality of water running off farm fields. Court rulings and federal regulations are apt to do it one day if Iowa doesn't act on its own.

The science about this isn't in dispute. Chemical runoff from farm fields in Iowa and the states around it has helped create a dead zone where the Mississippi River flows into the Gulf of Mexico.

It is a problem that Iowa can help fix.

However, the state's current approach puts the burden to act on farmers. We need to support farmers with a better approach—one that has farmers and landowners, the public sector and the private sector join forces to find a permanent solution.

It is just this kind of partnership that is now being tried in the Middle Cedar River Watershed above Cedar Rapids with a federal grant, a city of Cedar Rapids contribution, private-sector money, state expertise and the cooperation of farmers.

We in Cedar Rapids are involved for a good reason. We experienced a flood disaster in 2008 and a near flood disaster in 2016, and we also get our drinking water from shallow wells along the Cedar River. We'd like to see more runoff held on site and the water cleaned up that makes its way downstream. So it's our thought that doing the same thing when it comes to water in Iowa isn't enough.

Part of my focus on water stems from Cedar Rapids' special relationship with agriculture.

Surprisingly, my role as mayor makes me the manager of sorts for one of the largest farms in Linn County. That's because Cedar Rapids owns some 2,000 acres of farmland around the city's airport. And, yes, I've been out there on the tractor myself as the city puts its own water-quality improvement practices in place.

Each day, some 1,000 semi-trailer trucks loaded with corn and beans rumble into Cedar Rapids to deliver grain to the Cargill, ADM and Ingredion plants. More than 1.1 million bushels of corn are processed in the city each day.

I'm fond of saying that no city in Iowa is more tied to

agriculture and rural Iowa than Cedar Rapids.

During my time in the Iowa Legislature, there were years when both chambers were under one political party's control or the other party's control, and years when each party controlled a chamber. I worked with a Republican governor and a Democratic one. I was there when the state had big budget deficits and huge budget surpluses.

Through it all, legislators rarely made water quality a top priority.

In 2010, Iowans did pass an amendment to the state Constitution to force the state to use three-eighths of 1 percent of the state sales tax to fund the state's Natural Resources and Outdoor Recreation Trust Fund if the state sales tax is ever increased. However, the Legislature never has approved the money for the fund.

I've been proposing that the Iowa Legislature and governor do that—approve the three-eighths of 1 percent increase in the sales tax. The new revenue would provide a dedicated, sustainable flow of money to ensure that Iowa can better take on its water issues. Voluntary efforts now in place come with good intentions, but aren't enough. This isn't tax money to feed the belly of the state bureaucracy. It will fund the constitutional amendment that Iowans have approved and provide a much-needed remedy to a troublesome problem.

Like I said, Engage Iowa isn't talking about the easy sells.

But we Iowans long have thought ourselves stewards of the land and water, an identity that funding the natural resources trust fund will help preserve.

4

A BOYHOOD ALONG LAKE ERIE

My dad's name is Ron Corbett, too. He and my mother, Mary, avoided attaching "Junior" to my name even as they gave in to the custom of naming a son after a father.

Who wants to expose a first son to the risk of being nicknamed Junior? my dad says.

Instead, my family called me Ronnie Joe, throwing the short version of my middle name into the mix. My grandmother, who we called Little Ma, used Ronnie Joe until the end. She died just before Christmas 2016, at age 97.

My dad, the oldest of four kids, is the storyteller of the family, and he, like my mom, has lived a life of zigs and zags, with some ups and downs.

His life began on a small apple and pear farm close to Lake Erie just down the road from Erie, Pa. After high school and somewhat to his surprise, his grandmother paid to send him to Massachusetts to a strict-conservative, no-dance, Church of the Nazarene college to become a minister.

But he was back in Erie in less than two years. He eventually settled in as an industrial engineer at the Lord Corp.

factory, where he displayed a jack-of-all-trades knack that led to subsequent jobs in Newton, Iowa, and then in Amana, Iowa.

My mom, the oldest of eight children, grew up outside Erie, too, where her family had an acreage with peach and cherry trees. For a time, she thought she might become a Catholic nun, but she married my dad while in college instead, taught school and later became a nurse.

Like my mom and dad, I'm the oldest child. By the time I came along in October 1960 and my two sisters followed a few years later, we were living in a small house in a borough of a few hundred people west of Erie called Fairview, Pa.

My dad converted to my mother's religion, Catholicism, and I landed at St. John's Catholic Church elementary and middle school from grades 1 through 8.

I've not given much thought to how the nuns—Helena, Marguerite and all the others—shaped or misshaped me. Sister Marguerite knew how to rap us on the knuckles with a ruler if we misbehaved. But I can report no lasting ill effects. Among my toughest teachers was my mother, who taught my math and science class in fourth and fifth grades. She made me do my homework.

Fairview featured tar-and-chip streets with blocks of houses and an assortment of vacant lots where my buddies and I could learn baseball and football. I played baseball in the Little League and football, which I liked most, in the Little Gridders league.

My dad and mom were handy and hardworking, and they knew how to run things—my dad coordinated the Little League in the area—to fix things, grow flowers and tend a garden.

I remember as if it happened yesterday the evening my dad had me fill in as a baseball umpire. I was 11 or 12, and I had to make a close call on whether a ball was fair or foul. I still can hear the parents and grandparents from one team yelling at me when my call went against them. It bent me over and sent tears down my face. My dad called it a lesson learned. Sometimes you have to decide, he said.

All and all, I think my childhood and early adolescence qualified as what I've heard people call the quintessential American experience.

My mom took my two little sisters, Denise and Anita, and me grocery shopping at the end of the Friday workday, and if we were good, we all went to McDonald's for dinner. We looked each time to see if McDonald's had changed its sign out front that showed how many million more burgers it had sold.

We'd go to drive-in movies and help my grandmother pick and package apples from her trees to sell at the local fruit and vegetable stands. With Lake Erie just minutes away, we'd swim there and walk the beaches picking up smoothed pieces of collectible glass. It's called lake glass, and the glass is what the water has washed up from a time when communities dumped their trash into the lake.

My friends and I put pennies on the rail tracks that ran behind my grandmother's house and watched as the passing freight cars flattened Abe Lincoln's profile. We'd catch crayfish by hand in the creek, and around the Fourth of July, we'd marvel as my Uncle Matt tossed M-80 firecrackers into the water, sending minnows flying into the air.

I got my first kiss in fifth grade when Renee Rickard asked for one. It was conditional. I told her she had to promise that she wouldn't tell anyone. But with the milestone reached, she promptly ran around the school parking lot squealing, "Ronnie Corbett kissed me! Ronnie Corbett kissed me!"

I served as an altar boy in church when I was in fifth through eighth grades, sometimes alongside my mom's youngest brother, my Uncle Chuck. Just a year older than me, he called me Chubb because I was chubby. After one Sunday Mass, my uncle stuffed leftover communion wafers in his pocket right in front of me. I'm not sure if he was practicing to be a priest, but the next day he handed them to classmates as if they were in church taking communion. Of course, Father Carrick found out, and boy, he was mad.

The things we remember.

My dad ended up as mayor of tiny Fairview after neighbors insisted that someone other than the car dealer should run the town.

In the run-up to the election, he pasted together a campaign sign, propped it up on a trailer and parked the trailer around town. He had been active in the community, and people knew him. He was a Democrat because his dad was a Republican, and a Democrat at a good time, too. The Watergate hearings and Nixon impeachment proceedings were underway in Washington, D.C. My dad won by a whisker.

He was mayor for only a year or so. And no, I didn't run to be Cedar Rapids' mayor almost 40 years later because my dad once had been a mayor. In fact, I don't remember much about his time in office. I don't remember angry neighbors calling to get the snow plowed or insisting my dad quiet the yapping dogs. I imagine they did call, though.

At the time, my dad had hoped to win a transfer to his employer's new plant in Bowling Green, Ky. Instead, the company sent him to a training conference at the University of Wisconsin, where he accepted a job offer from a generator manufacturer, Winpower Inc., in Newton, Iowa.

My ninth-grade year of football had just ended in Pennsylvania, and that winter, we headed to Iowa. I was not going to be a Fairview Tiger, but a Newton Cardinal.

In the move, we left all my dad's and mom's relatives behind. I still can hear my grandmother, Little Ma, call our departure the saddest day of her life.

5

MY NEW IOWA HOMETOWN

I was 14 and on my way to becoming an Iowan. Little did I know that I would stay in Iowa for good.

My new hometown, Newton, was a manufacturing town like Erie, Pa., the place my family had left behind. So, Newton felt comfortable. My dad had traded up from one plant job to another. I still had my two younger sisters. And we had added a dog, Button, a Lhasa apso.

We moved into a two-story house on the northeast edge of town just a short walk to the junior high school. I was in ninth grade in the winter of 1974–75.

At the time, I considered myself something of a football player. But my new classmates hadn't had a chance to see a bigger version of me in shoulder pads, hitting and tackling, because I had played ninth-grade football back in Pennsylvania before our move to Iowa.

My Uncle Chuck was back in Pennsylvania, too, so I no longer had someone to call me Chubb. In short order, though, I got a new nickname, Wong. That's what the good basketball players started calling me when I kept shooting layups off the wrong foot. Wrong and Ron translated into Wong.

Quickly, too, I had my budding manhood tested when a kid challenged me to a fight. I hadn't ever been in a fight, and I didn't want to fight then. But for the better part of a week, I'd pass classmates in the hall and hear, "Bok, bok, bok, bok, bok." I guess it was my school's version of bullying. Whatever it was, it left me with no choice. I couldn't let myself be tagged a chicken.

So the fight was on. It took a couple of days to arrange, and after school in a backyard on the chosen day, a pack of young eyewitnesses encircled my rival and me, egging us on. To this day, I'm not sure what the fight was about. He was just a kid like me, a kid I didn't even know. I suppose I was new and needed to learn who was who in the school pecking order. In any event, I didn't get the chance to ask about it as I took off my Coke-bottle glasses.

The punch hit me between the eyes before I knew it, and sent me to my knees. Blood turned the white snow to red, and that was it. The fight was over. I didn't cry. Classmates Denny Griggs and Scott Van Zee, two good Samaritans, helped me up, walked me to a nearby Hy-Vee Food Store and cleaned me up in the restroom.

I went home, embarrassed, and lied to my dad, telling him I had taken one to the face in a friendly snowball fight. I didn't want to tell him about the real fight, and I didn't want to admit I had lost. I guess it all worked out. No one else tried to punch me.

In the years to come, I would get plenty of mileage out of that one punch to the face. In political speech after political speech, it was my fish story. Each time, my glasses got thicker, the punch quicker and harder, the blood redder in the snow. I've said it taught me to face problems, to get up when down and to try to be a friend myself.

24

By spring of my freshman year in high school, I was running on the track team. And in the fall of tenth grade, I earned a place as a running back on the sophomore football team. Track and football would help define my school calendar for the next three years. I joined the Fellowship of Christian Athletes and participated in the Junior Olympics.

I never professed to be a high school scholar, and sometimes I imagined I might work at the large local Maytag plant for the rest of my life. Newton was a company town then, and there wasn't a giant push in high school for everyone to go to college. Some of my classmates hoped for a job at the plant, following in the footsteps of their parents and grandparents. It was an option then. But for me, college increasingly figured in my plans as my success grew as a running back on the football team and hurdler on the track team.

I was pretty much on the straight and narrow in high school because I was always busy trying to stay in shape for sports. But I did have my moments.

As I got a little older, I figured out how to crawl out the window of my second-story bedroom late at night to visit friends without my parents knowing it. One time, a Newton police officer was called to a cemetery near my house where my cousin and I were trying to shoot squirrels with our BB guns. The officer took us home to my parents for shooting on private property. Another time, my friends and I were in a city park after hours, some were drinking, and we scattered into the timber when police arrived. I learned it's not easy running into the pitch-black woods in a panic.

I also remember one odd night at the drive-in movies with my girlfriend, and her mother was in the car with us. Her mother said she wanted to see "Grease," too. But I wonder.

I drove a used motorcycle, bagged groceries at the Hy-Vee Food Store 10 to 15 hours a week, and scooped First Avenue in my dad's steel blue Mustang during the summer. But that wasn't enough. I never did gain a following large enough to win the vote for senior class president. I was in the homecoming court, but I wasn't crowned the king.

Our football team just missed Iowa's AAAA high school playoffs in my junior year, 1976. But we were a powerhouse the next year, and we made it to the state championship game with me at fullback. We stalled near the goal line trying to tie the game when time ran out.

The year of our high school football success, I belonged to the business training program, Junior Achievement, and one of our businesses, which designed bumper stickers, fed off the community enthusiasm for our Newton Cardinals football team. We plastered "Red Pride" stickers on vehicle bumpers all over town. At $1 a pop.

To this day, "Red Pride" graces the water towers in Newton, a sentiment that the playoff football team and our bumper stickers helped to promote nearly 40 years ago.

In my subsequent careers in the Iowa Legislature, at the Cedar Rapids Area Chamber of Commerce and as mayor of Cedar Rapids, the challenge of drumming up support has sent my thoughts back many times to Newton, football and bumper stickers in that fall of 1977.

The following spring at the state track meet, I was competing in the hurdles when the Morningside College athletic director, Bud Brockman, approached me before one of my races. He asked me to play football for his college in Sioux City, though he knew I was headed to Cornell College in Mount Vernon to do just that in the fall. But he said I was making a mistake. Why play Division III football at Cornell when I could come to Morningside and play in a stronger Division II league?

Morningside also offered a full-tuition football scholarship, which amounted to about $5,300 a year. It was more financial aid than Cornell, which did not have athletic scholarships, could provide with other grants.

It probably was a big decision, choosing one school over another in different parts of Iowa. But I don't remember it that way. My dad long believed in making decisions, not dithering about them. So I guess I did the math, liked the idea of Division II football and picked Morningside. It helped, too, that a receiver on our high school football team, Dave Gullett, lived across the street from me in Newton, and he was going to Morningside to play football. That sealed the deal.

That summer, I played in the annual Iowa high school Shrine All-Star football game at Drake University, wearing number 32 on the winning South squad.

Then Dave and I packed up our stuff, loaded it into Dave's yellow Ford Galaxie 500, and headed northwest to Morningside for football camp before the start of school in the fall. I'd never been to Sioux City, but I liked it. I had no regrets, no second thoughts about Cornell College. I imagine I thought Morningside, with its tougher football competition, still might be my ticket to playing professional football one day. I was a dreamer.

6

WORK NEVER HURT A COLLEGE KID

I never studied advanced science in college like my son, Jeremy, who majored in biology.

Maybe he's right. Maybe I did carry an easier course load as a college business major, and so I had time to work during the school year and put in long hours at modest-paying jobs during the summers.

"But Papa," Jeremy would say, "I've got organic chemistry."

My son, like many college students and graduates these days, bemoans the load of debt that confronts him as he takes his early steps into the post-college work world. He is teaching English in elementary school in South Korea, and $200 of his $2,000-a-month salary is going toward paying college debt. I sympathize ... some.

I had financial help in my day, including a football scholarship to pay tuition for three of my four and one-half years of college and money from the Iowa Tuition Grant program. But I needed loans, too, even with the grants and money earned on jobs along the way.

I'm not sure how deep the debt from my college loans got, but I know I had to write a check every month to the

Iowa Student Liquidity Loan Corp. for most of a decade to pay it off.

I know, too, that it would have been worse but for the part-time jobs that never made it to my resume or long ago fell from it. I flipped burgers at a McDonald's restaurant; I pulled Saturday shifts at a storefront clothing store; I tended bar; I even worked the betting windows at race-tracks in South Dakota and Nebraska across the river from Sioux City and Morningside College.

The summer after my first year in college, I worked construction, riding my motorcycle from Newton each day to help build an elevator shaft and hang drywall for a library expansion in Grinnell, Iowa.

Late in my sophomore year at Morningside in 1979, one of my TKE fraternity brothers, Brian Wellendorf from Denison, Iowa, recruited several of us to join him on a magazine sales crew for the summer. He assured us that he had taken in a handsome few thousand dollars the summer before.

It was less awful than it sounds.

Our crew worked all the rural counties in northwest Iowa and some in southwest Minnesota. In each county, we started by going to the county recorder's office and obtaining plat maps by township and the names of each farm's owner. Then we went farm to farm, screen door to screen door, trying to get people to subscribe to magazines, particularly one geared to rural America called Capper's Weekly.

I had an old yellow pickup that summer, and I'd drive up to the farmhouse with the dust flying and the dogs barking to see what I could sell. Typically, someone was home, and I pitched the content of the magazines and explained that a piece of the profit would stay in the area to help local veterans.

I think Capper's cost $26 for a three-year subscription, and I got an $8.50 commission with each sale. People were nice about it. Many agreed to make a purchase.

Our crew could cover an entire county in a week or so, and then we'd push on to the next one: Ida. Cherokee. Buena Vista. O'Brien. Clay. Plymouth. Sioux. And on and on.

We'd stay, four to a room, at the cheapest motels we could find or at a local campground. Every day, we'd compete to see who could make $100 in commissions first, and we'd converge on the local tavern once we reached the goal. There we would play pitch or hearts and wait for the stragglers to return, some as late as 6 or 7 p.m.

It seemed the same people always came back first. Yeah, I was one of the top salesmen. I hustled. I was out there pushing hard, trying to work my way through school.

This is one of those back-in-my-day stories that parents often tell their children. I'm sure current students are out there working at part-time and summer jobs, too. I like that idea. I do think there is time available in a typical college student's week to earn some money, which might make the debt load a little lighter.

In fact, all five of my kids have worked some summers between school years, during the school year or both—even Jeremy, with the course load of organic chemistry and more.

Jeremy, who graduated from Wartburg College, worked at a coffee shop and a clothing warehouse and interned with the Iowa Department of Natural Resources studying crayfish in the Cedar River. Matthieu, now at the U.S. Naval Academy, worked at a Hy-Vee grocery store, a call center, Best Buy and a restaurant. Nicolas and Ana, both at Iowa State University, have worked as lifeguards and at restaurants. Nicolas also has worked at a radio station, and Ana at Hy-Vee and the ISU food service. (All four assure me this is an incomplete list.) Thomas, a junior at Washington High School in Cedar Rapids, works as a lifeguard. The older boys detasseled corn, too, with Matthieu lasting the longest: a week and a half.

In my time, it wasn't all dusty rural roads and sales charisma.

My buddies and I at Morningside College got caught up in a couple of get-rich-quick ideas that quickly fell apart.

One involved a chain letter that passed through Sioux City in 1979, asking that you put your name at the bottom of a 12-person list and send $50 to the name on the top.

Our friend, Jim Sjoerdsma, had signed on, and we thought he was crazy. But then he started getting money in the mail. We had student mailboxes at the time, and we'd go down and watch Jim open his. It would be jammed full, and out popped $50 from letter after letter as he opened them. So the rest of us had to try. I never made much. But some in Sioux City supposedly were making thousands. People had to hire security guards to watch their mailboxes. Or at least that was the story.

After that, my friends and I decided to try a curb-painting business where we would paint a homeowner's house number on the curb outside for a fee. But it was door-to-door work, some of the people weren't home and most of the rest weren't interested. It was one of those ideas that sounded better after a few beers than it proved to be out in the neighborhoods.

They say sales people are the easiest people to be sold.

And I guess I'm a sales person.

Much that I've done in my subsequent political life has involved taking ideas to the public and trying to sell them, even though the effort could come with a cost to me at the ballot box.

I've had wins and defeats in the Iowa Legislature, at the Cedar Rapids Area Chamber of Commerce and as mayor of Cedar Rapids.

But I'm still not afraid to try out an idea. What's the worst that can happen?

It's in that spirit that I've been traveling across Iowa since 2015 to talk about policy issues as part of Engage Iowa, the ideas initiative I founded.

It takes me back. It's not so different than those pleasant days out among the corn and beans, trying to make some money for college selling subscriptions to Capper's Weekly.

7

I MAJORED IN BUSINESS—
AND FOOTBALL

I'm not living in the distant past. Yet, I still have a few shoeboxes of yellowed newspaper clippings and tarnished medals and trophies from my playing days on the football field.

Funny, the boxes keep moving with me. I can't shake them, or the warm feelings held inside them. They stay, too, because they remind me of what it's like to be part of a team even as you're trying to stand out yourself.

For me, lifetime friends have come from football teams.

Denny Griggs was an offensive tackle on our Newton High School football team, opening holes for me so I could gain yards and some notice as a fullback. Now a U.S. Navy retiree, Denny helped plant a seed about military service in my son Matthieu, who now is in his second year at the U.S. Naval Academy.

Dave Gullett, another Newton High football player, and I packed up his yellow Ford and drove off to Morningside College and Sioux City, Iowa, sight unseen in late summer 1978. We leaned on each other as we made our initial foray into the bigger world.

Jim Sjoerdsma was a best friend on the Morningside

College football team and then on the football team at Cornell College, where we both finished our college careers. After graduation, we roomed together in Cedar Rapids before our marriages, went into a small business together for a time, and still compete against each other in middle age as we try to stay in shape.

Among the oldest of my newspaper clippings is a photo of me in big, black-rimmed glasses with my teammates on our summer-league Astros baseball team back in my boyhood home of Fairview, Pa.

There wasn't a team sport I didn't participate in as a kid, and that included my Saturday morning bowling team.

These days, I get a kick out of the National Football League's Play60 promotion that encourages parents in the digital age of social media to make sure their children play outside for 60 minutes a day. Growing up in the 1960s and early 1970s, I was playing outside all day long when not in school. Parents had to holler to get us back inside when it got dark. "Can we have another half an hour?" was the standard refrain. Usually, we could.

We had a good football team at Newton High School in my junior year and a great one my senior year when I was the team's starting fullback. But I wasn't the team's star running back. Halfback Jeff Girdner was. Colleges heavily recruited him, and he ended up playing at the University of Northern Iowa. I was in his shadow my entire senior year.

It didn't matter, though, that I was the second back. It still felt good. I was part of a winning team that competed in the state championship game for Iowa's biggest schools. What a dream for any high school player who loves football, even if you're defeated, as we were. There's something about football. Everybody has a role to play, and if everyone does it well, you can have a great team. And we did.

To this day, I've kept Morningside College's preseason football player guide for my first year there, 1978. The player guide features a long list of incoming freshman players, but it singles me out as the prized recruit. It also calls me, and only me, a top academic achiever. I'm not sure they got that last thing right.

I still have my Morningside helmet, too, which I've taken to speaking engagements in Sioux City and northwest Iowa over the years. What I don't have is a lot of fond memories of my playing days there. Our Morningside team wasn't good. In the two years I played there, the team was 2-8 and 0-10. That wasn't surprising. We were playing much bigger schools: North Dakota, North Dakota State, South Dakota and South Dakota State. I played some, and even started, but I don't have a bounty of press clippings from then.

In spring football practice during my sophomore year, I injured my knee, which forced me to sit out my junior year in red-shirt injury status. At the same time, the coach, Steve Miller, left Morningside for his alma mater, Cornell College, where he became an assistant coach.

After three years at Morningside, I decided to follow Miller for my last two years of college football eligibility. It was a twist of fate. I ended up at the school that I initially planned to attend.

At Cornell, I started as a backup to running back Barry Boyer, a friend of mine in Cedar Rapids today, who injured his knee during the first offensive series of the first game of the season. I'm not sure the head coach, Jerry Clark, even knew my name all that well when he pointed to me near the end of the bench and told me to take Barry's place.

That season I was the first Cornell running back to rush

for more than 1,000 yards in a season.

Playing football at a small college with a good academic reputation like Cornell doesn't make you a big man on campus like it might at Iowa or Iowa State, or even in high school. At Cornell, I wasn't walking around in my letter jacket, medals dangling, like I did at Newton High School. I had a letter jacket at Cornell, but I was wearing it to keep warm.

Running backs in football take their licks. And in my years as a fullback in high school and college, I pulled myself up from the turf wobbly and dazed more than a few times after a hard tackle.

But what I liked about running the ball was all the other times when you had the chance to avoid tackles or break loose from them. I wasn't one to lower my head and smack into the first defender I could find. No. After a split second to secure the ball in my arm, I raised my head so I could look downfield and gauge the shifting landscape of openings to run through and defenders to outwit.

During my senior year at Cornell, 1982, our team made it through the Midwest Conference undefeated, which landed us in the conference championship game. Headed into the big game, Coach Clark told the newspapers that "Ron can slide through the line, and he has the ability to run through arm tackles and go the distance, too."

Conference championship games matter, and we came so close to winning the one in 1982. The newspaper clipping tells it like I remember it. We were leading 14-13 over Ripon College of Wisconsin in the third quarter on my touchdown runs of 2 and 12 yards. But then we turned the ball over on downs inside the 1-yard line. Ripon came back to kick a field goal to win 16-14.

Suddenly, my college football career was over. Just like that.

Among the most telling memorabilia from my sports days are copies of two questionnaires I filled out shortly after my final season at Cornell. I sent one to the Dallas Cowboys of the National Football League and the other to the L.A. Express of the short-lived United States Football League. In my answers, I said my running-back strengths included good lateral movement and an ability to quickly get through a hole in the line. I could block and fake out defenders, too, I said.

I guess the questionnaires represented the last flicker of a dream about playing professional football, a dream that had begun in the Little Gridders football league back in adolescence.

There are other dreams. And with this one's passing, there wasn't any sadness. I wanted to play football and I did. Playing on after college was always the longest of shots. I don't think even Jerry Maguire—the sports agent played by actor Tom Cruise in the movie of the same name—could have helped. I wasn't fast enough.

I liked being on the offensive side in football. It requires initiative. You're always trying to move forward and to score. And I liked taking the ball with my head up, anticipating what was to come and where it made best sense to go. I've tried to retain that approach ever since.

Cornell College has its own athletic Hall of Fame, and the school has put me in it. The college's record books, as of the start of 2017, say I still hold Cornell season football records for rushing yards, 1,329 in 1982 (my 1,059 in 1981 is fourth-most in school history); rushing touchdowns, 21, in 1982; total touchdowns, 23, in 1982; and total points,

138, in 1982.

My numbers for rushing touchdowns and points in 1982 were best in the nation in Division III football. I was first team All-Midwest Conference that year and second team in 1981.

In the end, I was glad I started to pay more attention to academics at Cornell after long saying I was attending college to play football. I learned about business and economics and developed a liking for those specialties even as Cornell taught me that other lesson: You can't play football forever.

8

IT'S TIME FOR THE REAL WORLD

My mom and dad each bought me a briefcase as a college graduation gift.

They had divorced by the time I finished college in December 1982, so they didn't consult with each other on gifts. But what else was there to buy a graduate who majored in business?

Three years later, when I launched a dark-horse, yet successful political run for the Iowa House of Representatives, my campaign brochure featured a photo of me as I walked down a sidewalk in Cedar Rapids carrying one of the briefcases. I liked them equally.

Two briefcases bolstered my confidence only so much during the winter of 1982–83 as I took my first step from school into the real world with no certain job prospect in hand.

I didn't fear long months of joblessness, though, and I didn't worry that I would have to live off my parents or my friends. Granted, I sofa-surfed in their houses to ponder the big picture for a couple of weeks. But soon that was enough of that.

I returned to my boyhood home near Erie, Pa., where

my Uncle Ed thought he might have a job for me. I wanted to work. I was ready to get going, however inglorious the start might be.

My uncle, a lawyer, suggested I try helping in the office at a pallet manufacturing company, which was owned by a client of his and was having difficulties. I worked a week or so there, calling customers, including the DAD's Dog Food plant, to explain why their pallets had been delayed. But in the end, the company owner decided he didn't need a new office employee.

On my job-hunting trip to Erie, I brought along an application for a medical supply firm in the Midwest. I wanted to show it to my younger uncle, Chuck, to see what he thought. Unfortunately, a stray ash from his cigarette burned a hole in the paperwork as he was looking at it. Up against a deadline, I had to mail in the application, burn hole and all. I never did get an interview.

At the same time, my friend Brian Wellendorf, whom I had known at Morningside College, was working for the Equitable Life Insurance Co. in its Sioux City office and said the company had openings. I applied, got hired and had my request accepted to work in Cedar Rapids. I was familiar with Cedar Rapids, which is just down the highway from Cornell College, and a few friends from Cornell lived there.

By Feb. 1, a month into the job hunt, I had briefcases, a blue pinned-stripe suit and plenty of white shirts. I was set to sell insurance and investment plans.

I rented an apartment next to a bowling alley in northeast Cedar Rapids with my good friend Jim Sjoerdsma, who attended Morningside College and Cornell College with me. In short order, Jim added Peppy, a miniature schnauzer, as another roommate.

Before we knew it, though, the neighbors were complaining because Peppy barked all day while Jim and I were at work. Jim thought I should get a dog, too, so Peppy would have company and stop barking. On his advice, I bought my own miniature schnauzer and named him Buckwheat. However, the next day, the apartment manager let us know that instead of one dog barking, we had two. The dogs eventually learned to behave, and all four of us stayed put.

I was just 22, and both Jim and I had time to explore, looking for the ground floor of some business opportunity while holding down full-time jobs.

In one instance, Tim Brasel, a friend from my time at Morningside College, had moved to Colorado and signed on with a fast-growing, freeze-dried food company. We went to see him during his trip home to Denison, Iowa, so we could hear all about the company and the survivalist-like food it sold. We barely had time to sit down before he offered us a distributorship for the Cedar Rapids market.

As part of an introductory presentation, we watched as the packages of freeze-dried food—Swiss steak, beef stroganoff, macaroni and cheese and more—were dropped in boiling water or zapped in the microwave and magically transformed into food you could eat.

Jim and I could see only dollar signs as we imagined ourselves with truckloads of the packaged food to sell to young single men like us who didn't desire or know how to cook. Just pull this out of the cupboard and toss it in the microwave. You're all set. We were going to make millions, we thought.

But we didn't make it back to Cedar Rapids before Jim got sicker than a dog from eating so much of the stuff. Our quick-prep food dream ended along the side of a highway, Jim bent over, giving up the food and the fantasies he had taken in. I lost $80 on the project.

There were other short-lived ventures as we tried to find a path to the top of the business world. In one, we set out to establish a distributorship for foot care products. Jim and I held a couple of sales events in potential customers' living rooms, which featured, not facials, but what we called "footcials," or foot massages. The few I gave made me realize my future wasn't in feet.

We kept looking. Both of us had worked weekends at racetracks in South Dakota and Nebraska while attending nearby Morningside College in Sioux City. We figured we had sold tickets to bettors, so that meant we knew something about horses. Why, then, couldn't we make money investing in racehorses? The money wasn't in betting on horses, we realized, but in owning them. What could go wrong?

We each ponied up $2,500 to join a limited partnership that owned thoroughbreds. In turn, the partnership would send us photographs of our horses in the winner's circles at tracks in Florida and on the East Coast. Surrender Ground and Restless Rain were two of our winners. But all we ever saw were photographs. Once we began to ask about our winning money, the pretty pictures of winning horses stopped coming.

We didn't think we were stupid; we thought we were being cheated. So we filed a complaint with the office of newly elected Iowa Attorney General Tom Miller, and his office took our part. Miller's office found that the owners of the horse partnership had not registered it in Iowa, so the company had lured us to invest under false pretenses.

After a time, we got our $2,500 investments back.

By 1986, I decided to try another long shot to go with my full-time insurance job. I launched a campaign for a seat in the Iowa Legislature. I was 25.

9

WHY CAN'T I BE A LEGISLATOR?

The only election I had ever entered I lost. That was in 1977 when Lance Howe defeated me for senior class president at Newton Community High School. I can't remember why.

Nine years later, I had no good reason to think that it was time to test the electoral waters again or that I wouldn't sink if I tried.

That year, 1986, I was selling insurance and financial products for Equitable Life Insurance Co. in Cedar Rapids, and my colleague, Andy Anderson, was exploring the idea of running for the Iowa House of Representatives. I was going to be his campaign manager, whatever that meant.

But Andy got cold feet, not sure that he wanted to juggle a full-time job, two young children and a low-paying legislative post two and half hours away at the Statehouse in Des Moines.

I was single, so I said, "Why not me?"

After all, Andy and I had done all this preliminary work. Well, we knew who the incumbent was, we knew the election was in November, and we knew the legislative district at the time consisted of northeast Cedar Rapids,

Toddville, Center Point, Palo and Hiawatha. Then there was my brief stint as a volunteer in Linn County in the 1984 campaign for one-term Republican Sen. Roger Jepsen. He lost to Tom Harkin.

In other words, my own campaign announcement was a real shot in the dark.

A few weeks later, another young local Republican, Paul Pate, realized as much and entered the race. The battle was on. A third candidate, Darrell Walters Jr., also jumped in.

I quickly learned that a young, political neophyte like me was on his own until the June primary cleared the field and the state Republican Party knew who would take on the Democratic incumbent in November.

That forced me to adopt a primary strategy that was long on research and shoe leather, short on money.

I began by compiling a list of Republicans who voted in each of the three previous legislative primaries, 1984, 1982 and 1980. Then I knocked on the doors of these dependable voters, introduced myself and asked for a vote. I followed up with a postcard to each person I met. Then I went back and knocked on the doors a second time.

In truth, this was not a huge universe of voters. Only so many vote in primaries, and fewer still voted in each of the last three primaries.

My pitch in the living rooms and on the front porches was that I worked hard and I wanted to find ways to keep young Iowans in Iowa and to attract others to the state. That was my campaign theme: A Young Iowan Staying in Iowa. It seemed to click at that moment in time. Iowa was struggling in the wake of the mid-1980s farm crisis, and tens of thousands of residents were leaving the state.

Pate, who I didn't really know at the time, appeared to

be the odds-on favorite. He had been active in the Linn County Republican Party, and he had blanketed the district with campaign signs. Signs were a weak link for me. I couldn't afford them.

It was a surprise when I won the primary with 261 votes to Pate's 192. Walters came in third with 104 votes.

The result meant that fewer than 300 votes launched my political career, one that now has given me a 10-0 record in post-high-school elections. I've won one primary and seven legislative elections, six of which did not have primaries, and two non-partisan elections as mayor of Cedar Rapids.

It turned out that surviving the 1986 Republican primary was the easy part. In the November general election that year, I was facing Doris Peick, a larger-than-life labor leader with a sharp tongue. Among her labor supporters, she was fondly known as "Mother Peick." On top of that, Iowans for Tax Relief, a Republican-leaning lobbying group, backed her, too. The anti-tax group liked to support a few Democrats who had shown some sympathy for its stance on taxes, and this time Peick was one of them.

I did get some help. Del Stromer, the Republican minority leader in the Iowa House at the time, came to Cedar Rapids to campaign for me and to help me raise some campaign money. He spoke on a rainy night at the house of my supporters Ray and Phyllis Stefani, a house that I still remember for its lush white carpet. All I could focus on all night were the scores of wet footprints that dirtied that beautiful expanse of white.

In November, the election was a tight one. I won 4,609 votes to Peick's 4,356, just a 253-vote margin out of a total of almost 9,000 votes.

Slim enough was the margin that Peick asked for a recount. Fittingly, we had trouble agreeing on the makeup of the three-member recount board. She picked one member and I picked one, but a district court judge had to choose the third member. Peick also wanted a recount by hand, but the recount board, on a 2-1 vote, said a machine recount was sufficient.

The size of my victory declined by four votes to the final 253-vote margin.

It would be fair to say that my victory over labor leader Peick did not endear me at the time to her or to local union members.

She held no grudge, though.

Five years later, at the birth of my first child, Jeremy, Peick dropped off cloth diapers to my wife and me that she had made by hand. "You're a legislator. You can't afford disposable," she explained.

A year later, my wife and I had outgrown our apartment and ventured out to buy our first house. We liked a modest little bungalow next to Coe College and near a Dairy Queen, and at about $30,000, it was something we thought we could afford. We put in an offer only to discover that Peick owned it as a landlord. Go figure.

At the time, some of my income came from my part-time legislative salary, and in that year, 1992, the once-a-decade redistricting that followed the 1990 census count had thrown me into a face-off with another incumbent, Democrat Kay Halloran Chapman. It wasn't clear who was going to win, so the bank declined to give me a mortgage.

No problem, Peick said. She sold the house to us on contract.

It was a mixed blessing. Not a first day of a month

passed that she didn't call me at 7 a.m. to remind me that the house payment was due.

I ended up defeating Halloran Chapman, 8,979 votes to 6,577. Years later, she would follow Pate as Cedar Rapids mayor, and I would follow her in that job.

After my victory in 1992, I returned to the bank in short order and secured a mortgage to pay off my house contract with Peick.

I couldn't take another 7 a.m. call from her.

10

MR. CORBETT GOES TO THE STATEHOUSE

My worn-out Chevy Chevette hatchback made it the two and a half hours from Cedar Rapids to the Statehouse in Des Moines at the start of January 1987.

At age 26, I was the youngest Republican member in the Iowa House of Representatives.

Or put another way, I was "as green as grass," said Doris Peick, the incumbent I defeated.

I already had gotten a first clue that new faces didn't matter much when I attended briefings for the newly elected after the November vote.

I was reminded of that again when it came time to pick desks in the House chamber. House members choose desks by seniority, and I was the 98th or 99th among the 100 to pick mine.

The most-senior members take seats at the back of the chamber for a quick path to constituents and lobbyists roaming the Capitol rotunda. And for easy access to the restrooms. Newcomers land in the middle of the chamber. There you must climb over three or four other legislators and their clerks, desks and file cabinets to get to and from your seat. So once in place, you tended to stay put.

That first year, I sat next to Bill Royer from Page County in far southwestern Iowa, who was assigned to bring me along and show me the ropes. He helped.

Still, the first days are a bit puzzling. You shuffle off to one committee and another, someone is calling a meeting to order, and discussion starts on bills you've not yet looked at, let alone studied. But in a few days, you get your bearings.

In that first year, Democrats held a sizable House majority, 58-42, so they set the chamber's agenda, not us Republicans. And least of all me, one of the two newest Republicans.

Most of what I could do is stay true to my winning campaign theme, "A Young Iowan Staying in Iowa." And I pressed my legislative colleagues to look for ways to keep other young Iowans in the state. My presence as one of only two House members under age 30 sometimes made the point without me having to say much. I hoped they saw in me what Iowa needed to pay attention to.

My first committee assignments were ones I had requested: Commerce Committee, Education Committee and a budget subcommittee on economic development.

The two business-related choices made sense because I sold insurance in my full-time job, I was pro-business, and I wanted to see Iowa grow.

I picked the Education Committee because homeschool advocates had supported my election campaign, and in turn, I said I would study homeschooling as an educational option. At the time, Iowa limited the option, requiring that certified teachers do the teaching in homes. As a result, some homeschoolers felt they had to operate in the shadows. In fact, a minister and his wife landed in jail for a time for not following Iowa law. That didn't make sense.

My five children have attended public school, but I didn't think homeschoolers should be thrown in jail.

On that issue, we made some progress in my second year in the House, 1988, by passing legislation that prohibited jail terms for homeschool violations. Two years later, we passed a bill in the House to permit homeschool instruction by a competent, uncertified parent. The House bill failed in the Senate, but in 1991, the House, Senate and governor changed Iowa law to allow uncertified parents to homeschool if they were supervised by certified teachers.

In my first years at the Legislature, I stayed in a small room at the Kirkwood Hotel in downtown Des Moines and drove back to my apartment and my insurance job in Cedar Rapids when the session broke up for the week. I moved up from my Chevy Chevette to a rebuilt Chevy Cavalier, which eclipsed 300,000 miles going back and forth from home to the House chamber before I pulled the plates.

At the start of 1988, I learned that winning an initial election to the Iowa House didn't mean you'd win another one. First-term House members typically are targeted for defeat. And I was on particularly shaky ground because I was a Republican in a seat that had been held by a Democrat. In addition, my Democratic opponent, Cedar Rapids lawyer Gary Shea, was no slouch.

What I remember most about the race were the giant yard signs that Shea spread all over our legislative district. The signs weren't as big as billboards, but they seemed to be. It was hard to see the houses for his signs.

The signs were so large that they attracted the notice of Cedar Rapids code-enforcement officers, who said the behemoth size violated city sign rules. Shea questioned the city ruling, and I chimed in. I suggested that he should be running for City Council, not the Iowa House, so he could change the city's sign ordinance.

I won the election that November of 1988, 7,173 votes to 6,049. It was a win against a statewide tide that saw Democrat Michael Dukakis defeat George H.W. Bush in the presidential race in Iowa and Republicans lose three more seats in the Iowa House.

That meant that in 1989, my third year in the House, the majority for Democrats had grown to a 61-39 seat advantage. The numbers certainly didn't make it easier for a young Republican like me to be heard, which didn't suit me very well. I got antsy.

I decided I would show my colleagues that I was present and not just sitting around doing nothing. And I would have some fun along the way. My legislative colleague Brent Siegrist said I got a little "flaky" at one point. But I call it innovative.

It's true that proposed legislation is not like a page-turning thriller. Many evenings, though, I'd remain in the spacious House chamber, sometimes all alone, burrowing through bills slated for discussion to figure out a way as a minority member to amend and improve them. That could mean tacking on an idea that a Republican colleague or I already had pushed but that hadn't made it out of Democrat-controlled committees.

I didn't have much luck.

Nevertheless, it got so that House members would open their daily or weekly calendar book of proposed bills and amendments and see a long list of entries that read, "Proposed amendment by Corbett of Linn County," one after another. There he goes again, I'm sure some thought. Maybe I did get something of a reputation.

With every proposed amendment, its author gets the chance to stand at his desk, introduce the measure and explain its importance for five or 10 minutes. I was on my feet a lot. My colleagues weren't always listening, but I was talking.

Invariably, the House speaker would rule most of my amendments non-germane, and that was that. Early on, Don Avenson, a Democrat from Oelwein, Iowa, and House speaker in the late 1980s, let me make my way down to the well of the House to explain further why he and the House clerk should consider my amendment. Most times, the House clerk would shake his head, then Avenson would shake his head, and I would return, defeated, to my seat. At some point, Avenson began stopping me short and ruling against my amendment before I had a chance to budge. At other times, I'd just wave my hand in resignation and sit down.

Not every one of my proposals failed. One successful proposed change to the House rules called for a ban in the House chamber on the use of a legislative mainstay, the non-biodegradable Styrofoam cup. In another victory, my proposed amendment called for the installation of low-flush toilets in any state building under renovation or construction. Both amendments sounded like Democrat issues, not Republican ones, and that bothered Democrats. Here was a Republican introducing measures they should have introduced themselves.

During the Gulf War in 1991, I introduced an amendment to require the House to say the Pledge of Allegiance, an idea some Democrats called hyper-patriotic and even jingoistic. Civic clubs and organizations did it, why not us? I argued. But the majority Democrats accused me of playing politics with the war, and the measure died on a voice vote. I could have insisted on a roll call vote, so each member's vote would be known to the constituents back home. But I didn't. I wanted to prove that I had not been grandstanding and trying to exploit political sentiment at a time of war.

In the coming years, when Republicans won control of the House, sessions in the House chamber began with the Pledge of Allegiance, a practice that continues on Mondays today.

11

MY WIFE AND SENATOR BOB DOLE

I'm deeply indebted to former U.S. Sen. and past Republican presidential nominee Bob Dole.

But for Dole, I never would have met a young woman in France in 1987, or married her three years later.

I call it a storybook romance. Unfortunately, it didn't have a fairy tale ending. Bénédicte and I divorced in 2014.

I never imagined it would come to divorce when it all started.

Without knowing it, I positioned myself for marriage in November 1986 when I was elected to the Iowa House of Representatives just after my 26th birthday. At the start of the legislative session in January 1987, I was the youngest of the 42 Republicans in the 100-member House chamber.

In that year, too, the presidential campaign leading up to the February 1988 Iowa caucuses had picked up steam as Dole, the Senate minority leader at the time, was challenging incumbent Vice President George H.W. Bush for the Republican presidential nomination.

That spring, a Dole staff member called me and said the senator wanted me to be one of seven young Republicans from across the country to join seven young Democrats at a summer conference in Europe. It was sponsored by the Atlantic Council of Young Political Leaders.

I was flattered, I liked Dole and I even had had my photo taken with him. So, I signed on.

I'm not sure why I was picked for the European conference. Maybe someone in the Dole camp noticed something in me after I had defeated a Democratic incumbent in the fall of 1986. In any event, I was young and met that qualification of a program designed to teach young elected officials about the world. The idea was that we might survive the changing viewpoints of the voting public and one day become older political leaders.

The 10-day trip featured workshops and dinners with young politicians from several European countries. There also were sightseeing excursions, including ones to the World War I battlefield near Verdun, France, and to the champagne caves at Reims, France. An additional and unexpected attraction was one of the translators, a 22-year French woman, Bénédicte Agostini.

It wasn't love at first sight. In fact, I've long told her and others that I fell in love with her voice before I fell in love with her. She had a guitar and sang in a group during the trip.

Over 10 days, Bénédicte and I got to know each other well enough to agree to stay in contact once I returned to Iowa. But there was far from any guarantee that a relationship would blossom.

We were different. She was worldly; I wasn't. Her father was an international banker whose career had moved the family to Lebanon, Sudan, Portugal, England and France while Bénédicte was growing up. In fact, she had lived outside France more than in France by the time I met her.

As for me, the trip to Europe was my first outside the United States except for short family trips to Niagara Falls in Canada when I was a boy living near Erie, Pa.

Despite our contrasting upbringings, Bénédicte and I found that we liked each other. We stayed in touch inexpensively by mailing cassette tape recordings back and forth. Our cassette conversations were in English, which she spoke well, not in French, which I didn't speak.

The tapes led to visits. She came to Iowa with a friend, and I reciprocated, going back to France. We did that a couple of times. Then she returned to Iowa for an extended stay to get to know the state and for us to get to know each other better. That's when I asked her to marry me, more than two years after we had met. She agreed and returned to France to get ready for a wedding.

Five months later, I traveled to a small town in southern France, Puymeras, where Bénédicte's parents lived on a small acreage, to get married. An entourage of eight, including my mother, two aunts and three uncles, accompanied me. In France, the government requires a civil marriage ceremony, which often is followed by a church wedding. So we had a short civil ceremony officiated by the city's mayor, and a couple of hours later had a wedding in the local Catholic Church. I was married twice in one day.

As Bénédicte and I were leaving France for Iowa as newlyweds that year, 1990, I told her parents, "The next time you see me, I'll be speaking French." That next time, a year later, all I could say was "bonjour."

On the way back to Iowa, we stopped in my boyhood home of Fairview, Pa., near Erie, where my grandmother had a reception for us. Friends in Cedar Rapids did the same when we got back to Iowa.

It was generous of Bénédicte to agree to live in Iowa and not to insist that we live in France. At the same time, her decision made sense. She was so well-equipped to live in a new place, in the United States, because she had lived so many places growing up. I wasn't as prepared. It would have been a great leap for me to move to France.

My apartment—the one next to a bowling alley that I had shared with my good friend, Jim Sjoerdsma—became ours.

In 1991, Bénédicte and I had our first child, Jeremy, and every second year after that, our family grew. Matthieu was born in 1993, Nicolas in 1995, Anaelle in 1997 and Thomas in 1999.

All our children speak English and French, though I never learned French. It's one of those things I planned to do and wish I had done. Not knowing French sometimes got in my way.

As for Sen. Dole, I never encountered him in the years after my wedding to thank him for what he had helped to start.

12

SELLING ICE CREAM ON CITY STREETS

Iowa lore holds a special place for tinkerers who moonlight in sheds and barns out in the countryside, inventing the new and fixing the old and broken.

My good friend Jim Sjoerdsma and I were a little like tinkerers. Except we lived in town and weren't particularly good with our hands. So, we called on what we had—college business degrees and our wits. With that, we set out to find a start-up venture that would employ people and might blossom into something that made a profit.

Our early efforts hit far from the dart board. They included survival food for bachelors, a foot massage distributorship and an investment in thoroughbreds.

But we kept at it, founded a small business—a mobile ice cream enterprise—and labored to make it grow and prosper. Our darts were hitting the board.

It helped that Jim knew a little about ice cream.

During two summers in college when I sold magazines farm to farm in rural Iowa, Jim worked on a Stan's Ice Cream truck that crawled through neighborhoods in Chicago selling ice cream bars and other frozen confections.

Jim and I also knew each other well and so made good

business partners. We had attended college together, and by 1988, we had shared a Cedar Rapids apartment for five years, were single, had full-time jobs and miniature schnauzers, and imagined our big business break might yet come.

It was that winter in early 1988 when we decided to buy three used vans and to bring on a third business partner, Jim Turbett, who had handyman skills. He removed the side doors of the vans and built a sales counter in each of them.

We then had the vans painted white and came up with a neat company logo—a small girl leaning forward just enough to give her little dog a lick of her ice cream. The logo on the side of the vans heralded the company name, Peppy's, in tribute to Peppy, Jim's miniature schnauzer.

At the time, I was selling insurance for Equitable Life Insurance Co., and I also was heading into my second of 13 years as a House member in the Iowa Legislature. My partners worked at Rockwell Collins. Our signatures on a $35,000 small-business bank loan meant we would find time for Peppy's, too.

Before our fleet of three vans could take to the streets, we needed a chest freezer for each of them. No problem. We got a great deal on freezers at a going-out-of-business auction.

But we soon discovered that the bargain freezers didn't have "cold plates," which were needed so the freezers could keep ice cream frozen throughout a workday. Well, we had a fix for that. We bought and placed gasoline-powered generators in the vans to keep the freezers running. They ran. But the racket from the generators drove the drivers crazy and nearly drowned out the van's musical jingle that alerted kids that ice cream was coming.

So, we were two for two: bad freezers and generators

we couldn't use.

We also got a first lesson in the world of small business and government regulation. To our surprise, Cedar Rapids and Iowa City had ordinances that banned mobile vendors from selling on city streets. The thought was that small children would dart into traffic and get hurt or killed.

This sent me to the city council in each city to ask that the cities change their laws. One of the advantages of our membership in the International Association of Ice Cream Distributors and Vendors, aside from the annual conventions in Florida or California, was the help the organization provided in making our case. We persuaded the city councils that we had a right to use the public streets and that it would be an unnecessary restriction on free enterprise to deny our request.

Out into the world our ice cream vans finally went in the summer of 1988.

In that first summer, temperatures were at or near 100 degrees on 15 or more days. You'd think that would be a bonanza. But heat like that keeps people holed up in their houses, with the air conditioning on. It's a killer for the neighborhood ice cream business because the kids can't hear the van's music.

From the start, we found dependable, trustworthy drivers to operate the vans and sell the ice cream. In fact, the drivers made more money than us, the owners. What little profit we made, we put back into the business to upgrade equipment and hopefully expand. Sometimes I would drive on a weekend shift to make a little cash myself. I even competed with drivers to see who could sell the most in a couple of days. And I usually won.

By the end of the first year, partner Jim Turbett called

it quits, satisfied to take his name off the bank loan.

We ran our vans out of a garage in Palo, outside Cedar Rapids, so we could be next to Tri-County Dairy, where we bought our frozen products.

After the first couple of years, we expanded to seven vans, which operated in Cedar Rapids, Iowa City, Waterloo and some small towns in between. At the same time, we realized our ability to profit and expand further would require us to cut out the middleman, Tri-County Dairy. We needed to buy our products directly from the suppliers, Wells Blue Bunny in Le Mars, Iowa, and Meadow Gold in Des Moines.

However, to buy direct, we had to buy in bulk, and that meant we needed freezer capacity. So we moved our vans to a storage garage complex on the outskirts of Cedar Rapids and connected a semi-truck refrigeration trailer to the power in our leased garage. On delivery nights, we'd don insulated coveralls and move the ice cream from a supplier's refrigerated truck to ours.

The notion that we were on the right track, that we might yet become ice cream moguls, kept us at it. We began making plans to expand into Des Moines and other markets in Iowa, figuring we needed 30 to 50 vans if we really were going to make a go of it.

That's when we faced off with local government a second time.

The Linn County Planning and Zoning Department caught wind of our makeshift refrigeration operation and informed us that we couldn't run a permanent business out of a storage garage facility. I appealed to obtain a variance from the county regulation, but without success. The county officials were nice enough, though, to let us finish the ice cream season.

We renewed our relationship with Tri-County Dairy in Palo and rented out space from the dairy for our vans. But it was a setback, and time was passing.

In the November 1992 election, Republicans secured the majority in the Iowa House, and I sought and was named chairman of the important House Appropriations Committee. It meant I would be busier. At the same time, I changed full-time jobs, moving from Equitable Life Insurance Co. to trucking firm CRST Inc.

Something had to give, and for me, it was Peppy's. I signed over my company interest to my founding partner, Jim Sjoerdsma, in exchange for removing my name from the bank loan we had gotten when we started the business five years earlier.

Jim ran it another year and sold it to the owners of Tri-County Dairy. The dairy, in turn, sold it, and today, it continues to operate in Cedar Rapids and Eastern Iowa from its headquarters in Vinton, Iowa.

The fact that Peppy's trucks are still out there is gratifying, knowing that I was part of starting the business almost 30 years ago.

Since the beginning, thousands and thousands of kids—including my five children—have enjoyed buying the cherry-flavored torpedoes, the red, white and blue bomb pops, the fudge bars and all the rest.

At times over the years, I've heard the Peppy's jingle as one of the vans made its way through my neighborhood. And I've thought that the vans came and went too quickly. In fact, I've wanted to run out and tell the drivers as much. It's Sales 101 when it comes to ice cream. You need to inch along a neighborhood street to give the kids a chance. At first, parents tend to say no, but that jingle and the wonderful persistence of kids often can pry loose a couple of dollars for some ice cream.

During our biggest year, we had seven vans and 12 to 15 drivers, some earning money to pay for college. Nick AbouAssaly, a Cedar Rapids lawyer, and his brother, Mike, a physician in West Burlington, Iowa, both worked summers as drivers for Peppy's. Nick and I see each other these days in our roles of mayor, he in Marion and me, next door in Cedar Rapids.

My time at Peppy's gave me a hard-fought, firsthand view of the tribulations of starting a small business from scratch and working to make it a success.

In the years since, it has been commonplace for me as mayor, and earlier as head of the Cedar Rapids Area Chamber of Commerce, to say a few words as I've helped cut ribbons outside new businesses.

Those are always occasions to tell new owners how much the community appreciates their willingness to take the risk and put a signature on a bank loan.

13

DOORS OPEN AS HOUSE MAJORITY SHIFTS

I did what I could to matter during my first years in the Iowa House, with my dogged attempts to amend bills and incorporate minority Republican ideas into final legislation.

By the start of the 1990s, though, I increasingly focused on what had emerged as the central problem in state government—a nagging $408 million budget deficit. The debt was so deep that the state couldn't pay all its bills on time, including those to Iowa school districts.

Some of the state's money woes could be attributed to the lingering reach of the farm crisis of the mid-1980s, when farm values dropped, farms failed and a flood of young Iowans left the state. As far as I was concerned, though, the problem's cause was simpler: The government spent too much. The budget troubles didn't just happen. It was us, the Legislature and the governor.

The fiscal quagmire gave me and three other restless House Republicans something to grab on to.

Brent Siegrist of Council Bluffs, Steve Grubbs of Davenport, Mary Lundby of Marion and I had become good friends as well as like-thinking lawmakers with the idea that it wasn't enough to just say "no" to what Democrats wanted.

We saw ourselves as a band of sensible insurgents who realized, as many other Republicans did, that we could not accomplish much until we secured a Republican majority in the House.

At the start of the 1992 legislative session, Republicans held 45 of the 100 House seats, which represented progress. Two years before, we held only 39 seats. But the four of us wanted to do better.

And the decisions to come in that year's legislative action would help put a Republican House majority within reach.

That year was difficult, and it forced lawmakers to work into late June, through two special sessions, to balance the state budget. In the end, majorities in the House and Senate voted to increase the state sales tax from 4 cents to 5 cents on the dollar. Gov. Terry Branstad then signed the increase into law, calling it a "permanent solution" to the state's budget dilemma.

Grubbs, Lundby and I voted "no" on the sales-tax increase. I argued that the Legislature should have contained spending and raised some revenue by increasing the tax on cigarettes and wine coolers. Yes, wine coolers were popular then. I was not going to vote to pay for uncontrolled spending with a permanent sales-tax increase.

This sales-tax hike wasn't like local-option sales taxes, which voters must approve. Nor was it like my support in 2017 for a three-eighths of 1 percent increase in the Iowa sales tax to fund the voter-approved, state constitutional amendment that created the Natural Resources and Outdoor Recreation Trust Fund in 2010. Those sales taxes don't end up in the state general fund to be gobbled up by big government bureaucracy. They go for specific initiatives OK'd at the ballot box.

With the new state sales-tax increase in place in 1992, I headed out on the campaign trail with others, traveling the state for Republican candidates. I let voters know about the sales tax and encouraged Republican candidates every chance I got to denounce the tax increase.

We had some good Republican candidates that year, so the success of the legislative campaign wasn't resting solely on what I and others might contribute. And we had more campaign fodder than the sales-tax increase.

Iowa long had imposed a low annual registration fee on pickups, regardless of a truck's actual value, in deference to the state's farmers and their go-to vehicle. By 1992, though, this alluringly low fee was being enjoyed by a growing number of owners of minivans and sports utility vehicles. The 1992 Legislature kept the low fee for pickups but removed it for the others.

Grubbs and I voted against the fee hike. We both had young children, knew the fondness that families had for minivans and didn't want every soccer mom at the wheel to see her vehicle registration fee jump from $75 a year.

As we headed out to campaign, we obtained the state's public list of minivan owners broken down by legislative district, knowing that Iowans pay vehicle registration fees in the month of their birthday. Then we created a direct mail piece that targeted legislative districts with Democratic incumbents who supported the minivan fee increase.

"Is raising the fee on your minivan your idea of a nice birthday present for you and your family?" the mailer said. "The Democratic incumbent in your district thinks it is."

In our effort in 1992 to win a Republican majority in the

Iowa House, we also had to deal with the results of the 1990 Census and newly drawn legislative districts that reflected population shifts. The new lines put incumbent Republicans and incumbent Democrats into the same district in a handful of the 100 House election races, and we figured Republicans needed to win most of those to get a majority in the House.

That included me. I was in an incumbent-to-incumbent matchup. And I was hardly a shoo-in for victory.

With six years in the House, I was up against Kay Halloran Chapman, a 10-year House veteran, in District 52. The district now sat entirely in Cedar Rapids and had nearly an equal number of registered Democrats, Republicans and non-party voters.

These incumbent-on-incumbent races were unique because voters couldn't throw the bums out. An incumbent was going to win no matter what.

I campaigned as a foe of big government and against what I said were the tax-and-spend policies of the Democrat-controlled Legislature of the last decade. Halloran Chapman said she was a cost-cutter, too, as well as a lawmaker who sought compromise to fix problems.

We had a couple of good debates. She talked about childhood poverty, and she said the state should focus on helping poor families and not on the rhetoric of "family values."

I pointed out that the sales-tax increase, which she had voted for and I had opposed, would cost each family in Iowa about $300 more a year in taxes.

Halloran Chapman said the sales-tax increase was the best deal that lawmakers could work out to solve the state's budget problems. I said the state had to stop tapping into the pockets of taxpayers.

We also disagreed on crime legislation. She voted with the legislative majority to lessen the penalties for most burglars to help reduce the population of the state's overflowing prisons. I said the change would arm more burglars and put them back on the street more quickly to commit new crimes.

Surprisingly, I came out with an easy win, 8,979 votes to her 6,577.

Republicans also won most of the other head-to-head races.

After the math was done that election night in 1992, the Iowa House had 51 Republicans, 49 Democrats. We had done it. The House hadn't had a Republican majority since 1982. And as recently as 1990, the Democrats had enjoyed a 61-39 advantage.

The new Republican majority meant that Republicans now would chair the House committees. Siegrist, Grubbs, Lundby and I, the members of our self-proclaimed band of insurgents, moved into key positions. The Republican members of the House picked Siegrist, 39, as House majority leader, I was named chairman of the Appropriations Committee, and Grubbs became chairman of the House Education Committee. I was 32. He was 28. The top post, speaker of the House, went to Harold Van Maanen, 64, of Oskaloosa. Lundby, 44, was speaker pro tem.

In part, I had been rewarded because I helped Republicans win in the November election. Siegrist also pushed for me.

No doubt, some lobbyists in the Capitol rotunda were left to wonder a little when they heard that I, this pesky voice who was always trying to amend legislation, would be the new Appropriations Committee chairman. But I was more than amendments. I also had spent plenty of time on my feet, talking about too much spending, too much taxing and too little effort to balance the state's budget.

I had sought to lead the Appropriations Committee because that is where I thought I could have the biggest impact on the state's fiscal problems. I was committed to getting the state out of the red and back in the black. We were going to pay our bills on time, create a reserve fund and stop overcommitting on spending.

Within a few years, House Republicans would be sporting white T-shirts. On each was a graph showing a dive to a $408 million deficit, and the trajectory up toward what would become a $600 million budget surplus by 1996.

14

AL HAIG, JAY LENO
AND A SURPLUS

A squabble erupted at the start of the 1993 legislative session with me in the middle as the new House Appropriations Committee chairman.

The year before, lawmakers had promised to decide on the size of allowable spending growth for school districts in the first 30 days of the legislative session. That way, districts wouldn't have to guess for months if they would have enough money for their new budgets.

The self-imposed school-funding deadline created an opportunity for an early legislative victory to prove we were committed to fiscal reform. It didn't happen that way.

Early on, Republican Gov. Terry Branstad and the Democratic-controlled Senate settled on a school funding growth increase of 2.3 percent, or an additional $60 million. My Republican colleagues and I in the now-Republican-controlled House countered with a smaller increase of 1.6 percent, or about $49 million.

Making a point mattered as much as the actual money.

This was the first spending measure taken up in the 1993 session, and I wanted to make sure the governor and the Senate hadn't forgotten about the commitment to reduce the state's budget deficit.

"We're in control now," I declared at the time. "We're going to make the tough choices, and we're going to make them in the first week of the session."

One of my Democratic colleagues in the House took quick exception, saying I was having my Al Haig moment. I hadn't rushed in to declare, "As of now, I'm in control here in the White House," like Secretary of State Haig incorrectly did when President Ronald Reagan was shot in 1981. But I got the point. Maybe I was a little revved up. Still, I stuck to my beliefs.

The 30-day deadline for the allowable growth decision approached, and the sides still couldn't agree. The Senate moved its offer from 2.3 percent to 2.2 percent and then to 2.1 percent, while the House moved from 1.6 percent to 1.8 percent and then to 2 percent.

There the movement stopped, even though the difference between the chambers, which had started at about $11 million, was down to about $1 million.

I had been sick for three days, and I was gulping cough syrup on the evening of Feb. 11 as the school-funding deadline loomed at midnight. Meanwhile, back home in Cedar Rapids, my wife, Bénédicte, had just gone into labor with our second child. I delivered an ultimatum: A deal by 11 p.m., or I'm leaving. And I left. The deadline passed without an agreement.

Outside, a winter storm had hit, icing roads and closing some of Interstate 80 between Des Moines and Cedar Rapids. Thankfully, Sen. Paul Pate, also from the Cedar Rapids metro area, agreed to drive me home. I wouldn't have made it without him. The two-and-half-hour drive took five hours, but Pate got me there with a few hours to spare. My wife gave birth to a healthy boy, Matthieu. He was in much better shape than me—and the state budget back in Des Moines.

Two weeks later, the House Republicans agreed to go along with the Senate and increase the school allowable growth by 2.1 percent. Some of the money to fill the gap between the House and Senate proposals would come from "unspent balances" rather than new tax dollars to provide some face-saving for the House.

It's true that lawmakers and governors can dig themselves into positions and not budge. You negotiate day after day until at a certain point it gets silly to get so close to an agreement and not reach one. We had made our point. It wasn't going to be business as usual when it came to spending.

The 1993 Legislature was credited with balancing the state's budget for the first time in a decade as well as with putting an $80 million dent in the state debt.

Two leading political reporters at the time, David Yepsen of The Des Moines Register and Ken Sullivan of The Gazette in Cedar Rapids, credited Sen. Larry Murphy, a Democrat from Oelwein who headed the Senate Appropriations Committee, and me, the Republican chairman of the House Appropriations Committee, with working across party lines to deliver on the state budget agreement. Yepsen applauded us for setting aside partisan games for compromise and results.

Getting to a balanced budget, though, had its moments. With the House now in Republican hands, my ally Brent Siegrist, the House majority leader, and I, as Appropriations Committee chairman, figured we would get along fine with Gov. Branstad. We were all Republicans, and we saw eye to eye on a lot.

At the same time, Siegrist and I believed that Iowa had separate legislative, executive and judicial branches of government for a reason. For us, that meant we could have ideas and priorities that might differ from the governor's. We didn't need to wait for him to tell us what to think or do. My goal wasn't to make sure the governor liked me.

As the 1993 legislative session progressed, Siegrist, Branstad, a couple of other Republicans and I met in a closed-door session to discuss the budget. In his proposal, the governor had left out the cost of property-tax relief for lower-income senior citizens, which the Democrats had secured and he had agreed to as part of a sales-tax increase in the budget agreement of the year before. I said we didn't have a choice. We had to include the property-tax relief in this budget.

That January, Branstad was sledding with his son, Marcus, at a Des Moines golf course when a runaway sled struck the governor in the face, fracturing facial bones. The injury required surgery, which left his jaw wired shut for nearly a month.

The injury attracted the attention of late-night comic Jay Leno, who said the facial repair meant that the governor "may never be able to talk out of both sides of his mouth again." Maybe it's time to schedule sledding parties for all politicians, Leno joked.

The governor's jaw still was wired shut during our budget meeting when I reminded him of his agreement with Democrats from the year before.

He didn't like the reminder, I guess. He pounded the table and jumped out of his chair.

No one was quite sure what emerged in the mumbled thunder that came through the wires in his mouth. But I'm sure he accused me of being a "damn Democrat."

I jumped up and slapped the table in return, saying I wasn't the one who signed off on the budget deal from the summer before.

We sat down and figured it out.

I didn't have much time in early May to celebrate the state's first balanced budget in years before bad news hit. First came a summer of flooding across the state. Then the U.S. Supreme Court ruled that Iowa and other states should not have taxed federal pensions because they did not tax state pensions.

So much for the $48 million rainy day fund created by the Legislature in its just-completed 1993 session.

The floods of 1993 had started in northern Iowa in April, and by June into August, the rain and flooding produced the worst natural disaster in the state's history up until then.

"Iowa's Flood Disaster Report" on the 1993 floods estimated that floodwaters caused between $3 billion and $7 billion in damage, including $2 billion in lost crops and untold millions in losses to homes, businesses, public property and personal possessions. More than $1 billion was provided to flood victims through disaster assistance, and all 99 counties in Iowa were declared federal disaster areas.

Farm fields, little towns and big cities all were damaged. Chelsea, Iowa, a small town in Tama County, was flooded five times throughout the summer, while more than 250,000 residents in the Des Moines metro area went without safe drinking water for 19 days after floodwater inundated the area's water treatment plant.

It took until Oct. 1 before every major river in the state fell below flood stage, and by then it was unclear just how much money the state needed to find in its budget to pay flood-related bills.

Fortunately, the federal government agreed to increase its share of the cost to repair damage to public buildings and infrastructure from 75 percent to 90 percent. Even so, it looked like the state's share of the recovery costs would cut deep into the state's new, $48 million rainy day fund.

Little did I know how important these lessons about disaster would be. My role as House Appropriations Committee chairman during the statewide flooding in 1993 prepared me well, as mayor of Cedar Rapids, to help the city recover from a disastrous flood in 2008 and to help it avert a second flood catastrophe in 2016.

In the new year, 1994, the state's budget forecast showed that state spending controls and a healthy economy had combined to improve revenue projections. Consequently, we had enough cash to pay the Supreme Court-ordered tax refunds of some $40 million to federal pensioners without taking on new debt.

That spring would be a satisfying one in a Legislature in which both House and Senate chambers were on track to eliminate a state budget deficit that had reached $408 million in 1992.

Before summer, the Legislative Fiscal Bureau projected annual revenue growth for the state at 6.6 percent, up from an already robust projection of 5.9 percent.

We got another unexpected boost when changes in national accounting rules for state governments erased more than $200 million of the state's outstanding debt overnight.

At the close of the legislative session in late April, we had balanced the budget, erased the state deficit, built a cash reserve and created a Rebuild Iowa Infrastructure Fund (RIIF) so we could make repairs to the Statehouse and other state buildings.

I couldn't stop saying the one word that hadn't been spoken about the state budget for years. That word was "surplus."

15

A SQUEAKER ON THE WAY TO SPEAKER

1994 was a good year for Republicans in Iowa and across the nation. And for me, too.

U.S. Rep. Newt Gingrich from Georgia had ignited Republican hopes nationwide with his Contract for America plan to cut taxes, shrink government and dismantle welfare programs. Republicans also united around their disdain for President Bill Clinton's health care reform proposal.

It was a landslide year.

Republicans picked up 54 seats in the U.S. House of Representatives, giving Republicans a 230-204 seat majority, the party's first majority in the House since 1952. One of the pickups came in Iowa's 4th Congressional District, where newcomer Greg Ganske defeated 18-term Democrat Neal Smith. All five of Iowa's U.S. House members now were Republicans.

The story was the same in the U.S. Senate, where Republicans picked up eight seats to gain a 52-48 seat majority.

Back home in Iowa that year, Republicans didn't have to wait until November for some excitement.

Four-term U.S Rep. Fred Grandy, the former TV sitcom actor who starred for nine seasons on "The Love Boat," provided some celebrity color as he campaigned to unseat three-term Gov. Terry Branstad in the Republican primary. The primary race would turn out to be the toughest of Branstad's career.

In the hunt for votes, Grandy and Branstad climbed into motor homes and set out across Iowa.

Grandy labeled his city-to-city campaign the "Truth in Iowa Tour," and along the way, he chastised Branstad for the state's recent budget deficit and its inability to pay bills on time. He called Branstad "the MasterCard governor" who "cooked the books" to mask the state's budget woes.

Meanwhile, Branstad named his statewide tour the "Made in Iowa Tour," and asked Grandy why he was riding around in a motor home made in Indiana. Branstad's motor home was a Winnebago made in Iowa.

Branstad countered Grandy's criticism of the state's finances, saying as governor he had led Iowa through tough economic times and now had turned the state's budget deficit and economy around.

The governor and I had agreed on much over the years, even if we'd had our differences. Now I stood for him, and it mattered at a time when the two candidates were battling to land key party endorsements. Here I was, House Appropriations Committee chairman, vouching for the way Branstad had handled the budget. Branstad's campaign manager, Brian Kennedy, singled out my endorsement to the statewide news reporters as proof that top legislative Republicans had a strong working relationship with the governor.

Branstad went on to defeat Grandy in the primary,

winning 52 percent of the vote to Grandy's 48 percent. In November, he more easily beat Democrat Bonnie Campbell with 56.8 percent of the vote to her 41.6 percent.

I didn't have an opponent that year in my state House district, where I was on the ballot for a fifth two-year term.

Without a race of my own, I was free to travel the state to campaign for Republicans, including many first-time candidates I had helped identify and cajole into seeking office.

The campaign work paid off. We gained 13 Republican seats in the Iowa House, increasing our party's majority from 51-49 seats over the Democrats to 64-36.

No doubt, the so-called Gingrich-led Republican Revolution that swept the nation played some role in the surge of new Republicans in the Iowa House. At the same time, though, the makeup of the Iowa Senate remained the same, a 27-23 seat majority for Democrats. So, maybe my Republican colleagues and I, who had spent months talking up our House candidates across the state, had played a role in the new, large Iowa House majority. Maybe it wasn't all Gingrich.

With the election results in hand, I told my legislative colleagues that a strong wind of political change had blown in that doesn't come around very often. I didn't want to ignore it. At the same time, Branstad said his newly won term would be his last—which it was for that stage of his political career—and longtime House member Harold Van Maanen, the Republican speaker of the Iowa House, said this likely would be his last term as well. I didn't think it made sense to have a lame-duck governor and a lame-duck speaker at the same time.

I thought, too, about the campaign money I had helped to raise, the speeches I had given and the parades I had walked in. I had worked hard to secure a healthy Republican majority in the House, which is what I thought was needed for the Legislature to set more ambitious goals.

Among my priorities, I wanted to cut Iowa's income taxes, invest in new technology for Iowa's school kids and attend to the state's parks, trails and other quality-of-life attractions so young Iowans might stay in Iowa and others might want to move here.

So, with eight years in the House and two as House Appropriations Committee chairman to stand on, I decided to see how much goodwill my campaign legwork had generated. To the surprise of some, I challenged Van Maanen for the top leadership post in the House, the speakership. I was 34; he was 66.

The choice of speaker fell to the Republican House membership, which now numbered 64. That included 25 new members, some of whom appreciated the work I had done to help get them elected. Van Maanen and I each would need the backing of 33 of the 64 to win.

As the vote approached on Nov. 18, in a bold move, I asked Van Maanen, the sitting House speaker, to withdraw from the race. I told him he didn't have the votes.

Unfazed, he pulled out one of his little "blue cards," which listed the lineup of legislators and were used at the Statehouse to tally up votes on issues and bills. He looked at his card and counted 38 Republicans who promised to vote for him. In turn, I took one of my blue cards from my shirt pocket and counted 37 who backed me.

Obviously, with only 64 total votes, some of our colleagues hadn't made up their minds or didn't have the heart to tell us to our faces how they intended to vote.

I asked the speaker if he wanted to compare names on the vote cards, and he didn't. I'm not sure I wanted to either. To try and find the truth, I called on a few strong supporters to see if they could sort out fact from fiction. I figured they could talk to my shakiest supporters to see how they actually would vote. I never did get an assurance I would come out on top.

Every vote was going to count, so I was sympathetic but dismayed when my closest friend and ally in the House, Steve Grubbs of Davenport, called to tell me he was likely to miss the speakership vote. His wife was scheduled for major surgery at 11 a.m. the next day when the vote was to take place. Somehow, and fortunately, the surgery was moved to 7 a.m.

The morning of the vote, my Republican House colleagues and I met at a hotel on the west side of Des Moines for a lengthy breakfast. In a stroke of luck, a meeting room at the hotel where we had expected to convene and vote was not available. We had to reassemble downtown at the Capitol.

Even with that extra time, Grubbs still was nowhere to be found. Then I got another break. One of our longtime members suggested the new members take time to introduce themselves. They took time. Finally, Grubbs walked in.

By my calculation, Van Maanen had the backing of rural members and House veteran members, and I had support from younger members and urban members. As the secret ballots were opened, one by one, my opponent piled up an early lead. But I caught him at the end, winning by one vote, 32 to 31. The 64th Republican member, who would have voted for Van Maanen, was out of state and did not vote. My ally, Brent Siegrist, doubted I would have won a second round of voting.

At the time, news stories called my victory an ouster in an internal Republican power struggle. I'm not sure it was all that. Rather, I think the House Republicans got caught up in that year's gust of political change, too. It was a shift of power in the Republican fold to a younger generation. At the time, I was the youngest Iowa legislator to become House speaker. And as of 2017, I still hold that distinction.

Van Maanen credited me with outworking him.

At the time, too, he reflected on the turn of events two years earlier when he, as speaker, and Siegrist, as House majority leader, appointed me as chairman of the important House Appropriations Committee.

"When I named him appropriations chair, it was 'Ron who?'" Van Maanen said a few days after my win as speaker. "In two years, he blossomed and did a tremendous job, and darned if he didn't take my job away from me. Two years ago, he called me his mentor, and now I've got to bow to him."

16

NO WOODSHED,
BUT A BIG TAX CUT

Getting to be House speaker is just a start. My predecessor, Harold Van Maanen, suggested at the time that my successful effort to unseat him before the 1995 legislative session was designed to position me to run for governor or Congress.

That isn't true. I wanted to be speaker because I wanted to get things done. And the speaker's position was the best place to direct the House agenda. It meant that I more easily could put ideas into bills and then try to turn bills into law.

In my first days as speaker, I worked with other Republican leaders to modernize the House's habits to make them more family-friendly.

For instance, we moved back the workweek's starting time to noon or 1 p.m. on Monday so members could wait until Monday morning to drive to the Capitol in Des Moines. We also wanted members to be home in their districts on Fridays, which meant they would need to stay in Des Moines only three nights during most weeks of the legislative session. I thought the changes might make it easier for more people to contemplate a run for state office.

In another change, we provided better public notice of

the House's schedule so people knew when an issue was being discussed and voted on. We also wanted to make sure we conducted business in the daytime if possible and not in the middle of the night as sometimes had been the case. We wanted it to be the people's House, not just the lobbyists' House. Only lobbyists showed up late at night.

In another departure, my Republican colleagues and I had a baby-changing table installed in one of the House restrooms so House members who on occasion had infants in tow did not have to change diapers on the floor. The move got wide notice. It made it into papers as far away as Japan.

Believe it or not, in January 1995, I became the first person in the Legislature and in Iowa state government to use an Internet account for state business. People could reach me at speaker@legis.ia.gov. By February of that year, Sen. Tom Vilsack and Sen. Tony Bisignano, both Democrats, were complaining that I was using the Internet for political advantage. I suppose I was. They needed to catch up.

It is an overstatement to say that nothing moves ahead in the House without the speaker's approval. But it's probably true that the speaker needs to warm up to an idea if it is going to have any life.

As speaker, I wasn't a dictator. But I did try to make sure my Republican House colleagues kept their focus on the wide view. At the time, that meant trying to cut taxes and not overspending.

Another predecessor of mine as speaker, Don Avenson, a Democrat from Oelwein, had a more forceful style than me as well as something akin to a woodshed where he could take resistant lawmakers. As House speaker in the late

1980s, when I first arrived in the Legislature, Avenson would clean his fingernails with a bow knife one minute and pound the point of it into his desk the next to get someone's attention. Those were the stories, anyway.

I didn't have a woodshed. But I'm sure there were times when I exerted pressure.

In one instance, we were trying to wrap up the year's legislative session, and David Millage of Bettendorf, who was the Republican head of the House Appropriations Committee, and Larry Murphy of Oelwein, a Democrat who headed the Senate Appropriations Committee, couldn't reach an agreement on spending. Murphy asked me, as speaker, to help since we had worked well together in the past. And I did help. We reached an agreement when Millage took time off to run the Boston Marathon.

Being House speaker wasn't a big hug fest day after day. You have 100 House members, all elected by their constituents, and 50 senators, likewise elected, on the other side of the Capitol rotunda. Throw in the partisan nature of the place, and things can get difficult and complicated.

Luckily, the arrival of calves out on the farm helped us break deadlocks and reach compromises so we could get to the end of the year's legislative session. When the cows were calving, all the farmer-legislators needed to get home.

I tried to make a point as House speaker of finishing a year's legislative work during the annual session without the need for a special session afterward. There is a photo of each of the speakers in the back hallway to the House chamber, and underneath each is a list of sessions and special sessions over which each speaker presided. I like that there are no special sessions listed for me.

My goal as speaker was always the same. I wanted us to

be able to walk down the steps of the Capitol at session's end, in the light of day and not the dark of night, with smiles on our faces, knowing we had accomplished what we could.

In my first of five years as speaker, I pushed to put the Legislature on a spending diet so we would be in a position in the next few years to make what I believed was a necessary cut in Iowa's income-tax rates.

In 1995 and 1996, the House was controlled by Republicans and the Senate by Democrats, and it was my feeling as House speaker that we did more in the House than my legislative colleagues did in the Senate.

To prove my point, I worked to pass bills in the House in a punctual way so they could move to the Senate for its consideration. At several points during the 1995 and 1996 sessions, House Republicans donned green-and-white buttons that read, "Sitting in the Senate." That way everyone who visited the Statehouse knew the House was getting its job done. Anytime a constituent would ask about a bill, I'd answer, "Sitting in the Senate. Go ask them."

I also changed the name of legislative inaction from gridlock to Hornlock. It was my way of kidding Senate Majority Leader Wally Horn, a Democrat and friend of mine from Cedar Rapids, and to make the point that Horn and his fellow Democrats in the Senate were blocking the bills that the House had passed.

That fall of 1996, Republicans who ran for election used gridlock as ammunition to say the Senate led by Democrats had prevented the state from moving forward.

The idea apparently didn't hurt. In the 1996 elections,

Republicans kept control of the House and won control of the Senate.

An assortment of tax cuts along with budget surpluses were the hallmarks of the legislative sessions of 1995 and 1996. Any drama that developed wasn't enough to require a special session to make decisions.

At the close of the 1995 session, we had eliminated property taxes on new machinery and equipment to encourage companies to modernize and to attract out-of-state companies to move here. In addition, we had cut income taxes for pensioners and expanded income-tax deductions for dependents to lighten the tax load on families.

A year later, we closed the books on a $1 billion turnaround in the state's financial condition. In 1992, the state budget was $408 million in the red, and now, in 1996, the state's budget balance had reached $600 million.

There were a handful of reasons for the change in the budget's direction. Chief among them was the Legislature's decision to impose spending limits in 1992 that restricted spending to 99 percent of revenue. Other budget-bolstering factors included the increase in state sales tax from 4 percent to 5 percent in 1992; a relaxation of betting limits at state casinos and the addition of slot machines at racetracks, both of which increased state revenue from gaming; an infusion into Iowa of federal disaster funds after statewide flooding in 1993; and a change in national accounting standards, which permitted Iowa to clear more than $200 million from its deficit.

By mid-1996, Iowa's economy also was performing well, producing higher-than-expected revenue for the state.

So the stage was set. The health of the state's budget and the health of its economy cleared the way in 1997 for the Legislature to take up a top priority of mine and of Gov. Terry's Branstad's: a 15 percent, across-the-board income-tax cut.

At the start of the 1997 session, I told my Republican legislative colleagues it might be now or never for the tax cut. The next year was a gubernatorial election year, and I said there was the possibility that a Democrat might replace tax-cut proponent Branstad, who was not seeking re-election. In fact, a Democrat, Tom Vilsack, did replace him.

Early in the 1997 legislative session, the House quickly passed the 15 percent income-tax cut, only to see the Iowa Senate hesitate. The Senate scaled back the proposal to a 10 percent cut, which would save Iowans about $200 million a year, not the $300 million a year with the 15 percent cut.

I didn't quickly give up on the 15 percent proposal. But passing any sizable income-tax cut is difficult. It's hard to make the case with a Capitol rotunda filled day in and day out with interest groups from across the state that depend on state tax revenue. The beneficiaries of a tax cut are back home, getting up and going to work. They're not at the Capitol. Groups like Iowans for Tax Relief could help only so much.

In the end, the Republican majority in the House agreed to the Senate's 10 percent cut.

The 10 percent cut lowered Iowa's top income-tax rate from 9.98 percent to 8.98 percent, where it sits today, still fourth-highest among the 50 states. Deductions, which include deductibility for federal income tax payments, make Iowa's effective tax rates lower. Even so, the perception is that the rates are high and, in my mind, this dissuades companies and people from moving to or staying in Iowa.

Little has changed since. In 2017, it will be 20 years since Iowa did anything of significance to improve its income-tax code. I'm in favor of modernizing and simplifying the code so the state's income-tax rates don't seem higher than they are. I don't want to scare employers and workers away. I want to keep them and attract more of them.

MOM AND DAD: **Top:** Mom with (left to right) my sister Denise, me and my sister Anita at the Erie, Pa., zoo. **Bottom:** Dad runs for mayor, Fairview, Pa., 1973.

SPORTS: Top: Little League baseball: I'm in the Astros uniform and black glasses.

Left: My success as a Cornell College running back began with (above) Little Gridders football.

MY POLITICAL CAREER STARTS: Incumbent Doris Peick and I face off one last time in 1986—in front of a Linn County recount board.

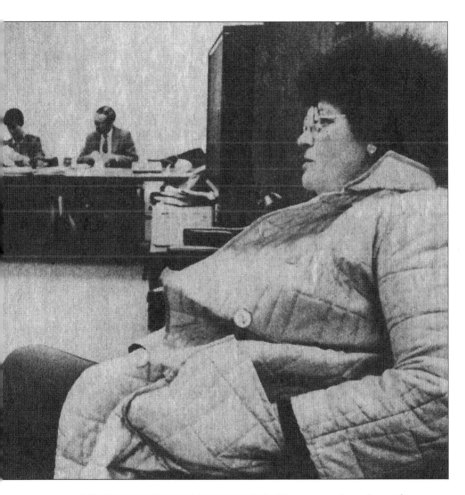

MY FIRST ELECTION VICTORY: The recount board certifies my election to the Iowa House of Representatives by a thin, 253-vote margin. Doris didn't hold a grudge.

AN IOWA LEGISLATOR: **Top:** My new colleagues and I in the Iowa House take the oath of office, January 1987. **Below left:** With U.S. Rep. Newt Gingrich, 1994. Below right: With U.S. Sen. Bob Dole, 1987.

Best Wishes, Ron
from Chuck Grassley
your Senator
" congratulations, Mr. Speaker ! "
12-20-94

SPEAKER OF THE HOUSE: I stop at Sen. Chuck Grassley's farm in December 1994 for advice after being selected as House speaker by my Republican colleagues in the House.

CHAMBER OF COMMERCE: Top: Larry Murphy, consultant and former state senator, and I review the vote victory of the Support Our Schools building campaign in Cedar Rapids, 2000. **Bottom:** Former Gov. Bob Ray comes to Cedar Rapids to promote the Iowa Child rain forest project, 2001. (From right): Project founder Ted Townsend, Ray, Mayor Lee Clancey and me, head of the Chamber of Commerce.

ELECTED MAYOR: Top: Mayoral candidates threw darts to see who would answer debate questions first. **Bottom:** My son, Thomas, helps celebrate victory, 2009.

THE 2008 FLOOD: **Top:** Only boats could use downtown Cedar Rapids' main thoroughfare. **Bottom:** Floodwater ripped harbor houses from their moorings in the Ellis Park boat harbor and stacked them against a rail bridge across from the Quaker Oats plant.

FIVE YEARS LATER: **Top:** The Veterans Memorial Building on June 13, 2008, during the flood. **Bottom:** The fifth anniversary commemoration of the flood on May's Island in front of the Vets building, the former City Hall.

REBUILDING: Top: As mayor, I push the explosives button in July 2011 that brings down an old parking ramp to make way for the city's convention center. Bottom: The dedication of the city's new downtown library, August 2013. The old one was ruined in the 2008 flood.

D.C. COMES TO CEDAR RAPIDS: Top: U.S. Rep. Dave Loebsack helps rededicate the renovated Grant Wood-designed stained glass window at the Veterans Memorial Building, July 4, 2010. **Bottom:** President Barack Obama visits a Cedar Rapids manufacturing plant, 2012. (From right) Gov. Terry Branstad, me, U.S. Reps. Loebsack and Bruce Braley. Federal funding for flood recovery and protection always was a topic for discussion when federal officeholders came to town.

WATER QUALITY & BIOFUEL: We're planting deep-rooted grass on city-owned farmland at The Eastern Iowa Airport. The Miscanthus grass retains water in the field and is harvested as a biofuel.

SOME OF MY CONSTITUENTS:
Top: I invited homeless men and women and advocates to City Hall to talk about safety and winter shelter, 2015.
Bottom: Reading during Week of the Young Child, 2014.

DUTIES OF MAYOR: Top: Circus elephants get the key to the city. Bottom: Annual mayoral bike ride (left), and a run along city streets prior to a vote on street repairs (right). All photos, fall of 2013.

LOSE AND WIN: Top: I'm the tour guide, showing the Racing and Gaming Commission the site of the proposed Cedar Rapids casino, 2014. It was voted down. **Bottom:** I explain Cedar Rapids' sales tax-sharing plan at the Statehouse, 2011. The plan to help pay for flood protection succeeded.

HOLDING BACK A FLOOD 2016: Gov. Terry Branstad (to my right), Lt. Gov. Kim Reynolds and U.S. Rep. Rod Blum (to my left) watch with me as emergency crews fill HESCO barriers with sand (**see middle photo, right page**) to hold back the flooding Cedar River, September 2016.

VICTORY: Left: Volunteers celebrate with Jason Lester, Paramount Theatre event manager. As a precaution against flooding, they removed the theatre's first-floor seats. But water didn't enter as it did in the 2008 flood.

A CHALLENGE: Left: I asked residents to support businesses when they reopened after the flood scare. I did, at Sykora Bakery.
Above: Filling HESCO barriers.

17

MY MOM, CRACK
AND THE DEATH PENALTY

My mom taught me how to open a can of Spam® with that little key on the side and how to fry baloney and watch as it curled up at the edges.

She helped tame a cowlick in my hair until she thought I looked good. And she showed me how to weed a flower garden and iron a shirt.

She's been there for me.

But children grow up and parents age, and they can fall out of close contact amid the demands of adult life.

In 1993, my wife and I had our own young family. I was holding down a full-time job in Cedar Rapids and serving in the Iowa Legislature as chairman of the Iowa House Appropriations Committee. And by then, my mom and dad had divorced and she had moved back east, where most of her family lived.

So I was surprised when my mom started calling me at the Statehouse in early 1993.

"Ronnie, I need some money for food," the voice on the phone pleaded. "I haven't eaten for three days." She sounded desperate. Of course, I wired her money, and more calls followed.

"Ronnie, you're my son. I've done everything for you, and I need some help now," she would say.

Before long, her brother, my Uncle Ed, told me to stop. He said she wasn't using the money for food. She was buying drugs. She needed to hit bottom, he told me.

So, I stopped, and she hit bottom.

I'm still not sure how it had come to this.

My mom was the oldest of eight children and had considered becoming a nun. She taught science and math classes in my Catholic elementary school near my boyhood home of Fairview, Pa., before we moved to Newton, Iowa, in late 1974.

I was in college in 1981 when my mom and dad divorced, so I didn't know all the details of their breakup. But she picked up the pieces and worked to carve out a new life for herself.

She made the 60-mile round trip from Newton to the community college in Marshalltown most days for a couple of years to earn a nursing degree. Then, to get a fresh start, she moved to the Washington, D.C., area to live for a time with one of her brothers and his wife and to begin a new job as a nurse.

At some point, she—a middle-aged nurse and grandmother—started a relationship with a man who had had substance abuse problems. Before long, he introduced her, a lifelong smoker, to crack cocaine. Casual use led to crack cocaine parties and then to abuse. She burned through her savings, retirement money and lines of credit and did all the things that people addicted to drugs do.

Including begging a son for money.

Then one day, her boyfriend found her in a bathroom, lying on the floor. An ambulance took her to the hospital, and eventually, she made her way to addiction treatment.

I didn't expect to publicly reveal the story of my mom's descent into addiction and her recovery from it, let alone see it make the front page of newspapers.

But it did, five years after her desperate phone calls to me.

Her story slipped out in mid-February 1998 as I was venting my frustration to a visiting delegation of community leaders about the Legislature's unwillingness to restore the death penalty for certain crimes.

I told them that Iowa not only needed more prison beds, but it could benefit from the death penalty. I added that I might even consider capital punishment for certain big-time drug dealers and manufacturers whose crimes resulted in the death of drug users. Before I knew it, I was telling the story of my mom's drug addiction, downward spiral and subsequent recovery.

I told them it had been tough seeing her destroy her life. Just think what can happen to youngsters if my mom, who was older and educated, could fall into the addiction trap, I said.

I said we needed to better educate Iowans about addiction, help those addicted get help and get tough with those who deal illegal drugs.

There were no news reporters present when I talked that evening after the day's legislative session, but word made its way to them about my mom and crack cocaine.

The news stories that followed prompted many people to call me and send me notes. A few chastised me for not calling police and turning my mother in. But most were kind.

It's surprising how many people deal with addiction in their lives, whether it is their addiction or that of a family member or a friend. Some told me that my mom's story comforted them. It made them feel less alone knowing that others had gone through what they had.

My mom didn't like that I had talked about our family secret in public. In time, though, she forgave me.

She was lucky. She came close to dying, wasted her life's savings and nearly lost her nurse's license. But she made it back, left the drugs behind and worked as a nurse until she retired.

Just a few days before I let her story slip out in 1998, I, as speaker of the Iowa House, pulled the plug on a proposed death penalty bill. I didn't have 51 of 100 votes in the House to support it, and it was clear that the Iowa Senate would oppose the bill.

A month before, I thought I had the votes, in the House at least. But that changed after death-penalty foes, including Dubuque Archbishop Jerome Hanus and Iowa Attorney General Tom Miller, crowded into the Statehouse to urge lawmakers to reject capital punishment.

Another factor at the time was the execution of a woman for murder in Texas in what was the first execution of a female in the United States since 1984. Some of my legislative colleagues who had not made up their minds on the death penalty now did.

"When they were confronted with the actual reality that a woman could be put to death just like a man, that caused some concern for some members who were on the bubble," I said at the time.

The death penalty defeat in the Legislature in 1998 shouldn't have surprised me. It was a repeat of a defeat three years earlier.

In 1995, my first year as House speaker, I, along with Gov. Terry Branstad, backed a bill to restore capital punishment on a limited basis. The House voted 54-44 to lift the ban on the death penalty put in place by Iowa lawmakers and Gov. Harold Hughes in 1965. However, the Senate rejected the idea, 39-11.

The defeats on capital punishment didn't mean legislators and the governor didn't get tougher on crime and the type of criminals that my mother had fallen victim to. In the last half of the 1990s, we agreed to build three new prisons and to add on to two others.

If I were asked today, I'd advise Iowa lawmakers to forget about changing Iowa law to allow for the death penalty. The ban in Iowa has been in place now for more than 50 years, and the state has moved well beyond the issue. Two efforts in 1995 and 1998 to set the ban aside came to naught. And in both years, the debates took up so much time and generated so much emotion that other important legislative matters were pushed to the side.

I still think the death penalty can make sense in extraordinary cases, but not every issue is clear-cut. Lawmakers risk gridlock if they can't see the gray between the black and white, the yes and no.

The death penalty strikes a nerve in people. When we debated the issue in 1995, every one of the 100 House members came to the microphone to weigh in.

Death is final, and there is a part in most people, whether religious or not, that believes redemption is possible, that someone can change. Life in prison can allow for that. Execution can't.

18

EDUCATION REFORM FLAMES OUT

I played football in my day, and knew how players poured Gatorade on head coaches after a big victory. So I was lining up a load of the fitness drink at the start of the legislative session in January 1998.

If the 1997 session featured a big income-tax cut, the 1998 session was set to become a triumph of state education reform for Gov. Terry Branstad in his final year of 16 years in office. His education initiative for grades kindergarten through 12 had legacy written all over it.

"If you do nothing else this year, do not leave here without reforming our schools," Branstad said in his Condition of the State speech that year. "... If we fail to act now, our kids will forever suffer."

The lofty language only went so far.

Broad education reform didn't happen in 1998, despite a Republican governor with a Republican-controlled Legislature. Republicans had a 55-45 majority in the House and a 27-22 majority in the Senate. But lawmakers and the governor just couldn't agree on every detail of the reform legislation.

Branstad had put education reform at the top of his

agenda the year before when he appointed a Commission on Educational Excellence for the 21st Century, headed by Des Moines businessman Marvin Pomerantz. The commission issued its report later in 1997, and its recommendations formed the core of Branstad's education reform proposals that he wanted the Legislature to pass in the 1998 session.

Reforms were needed. Iowa was seeing declining test scores for elementary students while concern was growing that too few college students were turning to the teaching profession because of low pay.

The governor's education reform package called for increased starting pay for teachers, improved teacher training, merit pay increases for good teachers, new accountability standards for schools and better early childhood development programs.

Pomerantz told lawmakers that strengthening the teaching profession was the most important of the commission's recommendations.

In my opening remarks to the Iowa House as speaker that year, I agreed with the governor, saying we should pay teachers more, put more accountability into the school system and help low-income families send their children to preschool.

But I cautioned, too, that the Legislature and governor needed to take care that they weren't telling local schools, parents and children that only Des Moines knows best on school matters.

Reaching any agreement on education reform also had to consider the differing needs and thinking of rural and urban schools as well as the issues of class size, school infrastructure repairs and tax relief for parents who send children to private schools.

House Majority Leader Brent Siegrist and I had some of our own education reform priorities, too.

The two of us had traveled to Murfreesboro, Tenn., in late 1997 to tour Lane Academy along with Lamar Alexander, who today is a U.S. senator as well as a former Tennessee governor and former U.S. secretary of education. We liked what we saw. The school, a unique, year-round charter school, was premised on the idea that students also can thrive in studies and activities outside traditional school hours. The school featured short-term "camps" to study special subjects during breaks in the school year.

Siegrist and I brought the idea back with us and included a proposal for cutting-edge "frontier" schools in the 1998 education reform legislation. We wanted to encourage Iowa communities to innovate.

But by mid-March and well past the midpoint of the legislative session, nothing looked certain about education reform.

As House speaker, I found myself trying to prevent an impending train wreck as House Republicans declined to support certain provisions of Branstad's education reform package.

Some urban lawmakers, for instance, opposed raising the minimum teacher salary from $18,000 to $23,000 a year because they thought it would benefit rural districts most. Urban districts already were paying at the higher salary level, so they wouldn't gain anything. Others did not support spending $9 million a year for merit pay for teachers, which the governor wanted.

Along the way, Branstad got his money for minimum teacher salaries, and, as far as I was concerned, he secured much of the rest of what he wanted from the Legislature. He didn't see it that way.

In the waning days of the session, the governor threatened to veto the legislation and call a special session if we didn't fix the reform package. He said we had failed on many of the proposals spelled out in the Pomerantz commission recommendations.

"... (T)his bill falls far short of the needed reforms," he said with his veto threat pending. "The children of Iowa deserve better, and I intend to see that they get it."

Meanwhile, I was scurrying around in a last-ditch attempt to add $3.7 million to the bill for merit pay for teachers. But Branstad said the bill had many more problems than that.

To this day, Siegrist recalls the moment when Branstad suddenly appeared on the House floor, which he rarely if ever had done, as lawmakers were taking turns giving farewell addresses and preparing to go home for the year. The governor insisted on talking directly to all the House Republicans, not just to us leaders. And he wanted to talk right then.

Siegrist and I sat silent and listened as our rank-and-file Republican colleagues told Branstad what they were and weren't willing to support.

At the time, I compared the governor to a football coach calling time out with 30 seconds left in the game— while his players were ready to throw Gatorade on him and carry him off the field—to yell because his team was winning 21-0 and not 28-0.

"It's his last trump card he has to play, this veto threat

to the Legislature," I said.

And the governor played it. He used his line-veto power to ax $17.4 million from the $24 million educational reform bill sent to him by the Legislature.

In a 2015 biography, "Iowa's Record Setting Governor: The Terry Branstad Story," Branstad said he did not want his reform package passed piecemeal, and he said that is what the Legislature did.

Among what he vetoed from the education bill were block grants that left it to school districts to decide how to improve elementary school programs. He favored targeted reforms proposed by the education commission, not the block-grant approach.

He also vetoed money to help school districts with growing enrollments and those with declining enrollments; merit pay for teachers because the amount in the legislation was short of what he wanted; and an initiative to exempt "frontier" schools from state regulations. The latter was the idea proposed by Siegrist and me.

Surviving in the legislation were an increase in beginning teachers' salaries, a $5.2 million increase in early childhood education programs and legislative language that made it easier to fire teachers doing substandard work.

Branstad tried to persuade lawmakers to return for a special session to redo the education reform measure. But no special session ever happened.

Senate Majority Leader Stewart Iverson, a Republican from Dows, Iowa, made it clear at the time that the disagreement with Branstad wasn't only with Siegrist and me and our Republican colleagues in the House. Senate Republicans weren't on board with the governor either.

"Our people compromised a long way to get this bill,"

Iverson said after Branstad's veto and his call for a special session. "I don't see any more compromising at this point. He's not hurting legislators. He's hurting the schoolchildren of Iowa."

Branstad said it was the Legislature that was to blame for our "halting, half steps toward education reform."

In the big picture, the education reform debate in 1998 was a healthy one and foreshadowed coming national debates on reforms imposed from the top down, such as No Child Left Behind and the Common Core Educational Standards Initiative.

In 1998, the concern about infringement on local school district control was a hurdle that the governor's reform package couldn't get over.

I think subsequent reforms that have trickled down from the federal government have zapped innovation from local school districts and buried schools and teachers in too many regulations. I want to go in the opposite direction.

At the close of the 1998 legislative session, I remember Branstad held a news conference with some Democrats to make the case for his education proposal and to call out Republican lawmakers for not agreeing to a special session.

"Right now, Republicans are acting out of anger. They should cool off," Democrat Mike Gronstal, the Senate minority leader from Council Bluffs, said at the time, standing shoulder to shoulder with Branstad.

In turn, Siegrist and I spoke on a few radio ads to defend the Iowa House and to say that we had gotten from lawmakers all that we could get.

June came, and both Republicans and Democrats

focused on contested gubernatorial primaries. After that, people were looking beyond Branstad to who would replace him: Democrat Tom Vilsack, a state senator, or U.S. Rep. Jim Ross Lightfoot, a Republican.

In the end, we all felt bad that more could not have been accomplished on education reform in 1998. It just wasn't the way to send the governor out after 16 years in office. We were elected officials, and we knew how hard it is to be governor and how hard he worked.

We did want to douse the coach with Gatorade and carry him off the field. We just weren't able. It left a bad taste in everyone's mouth.

19

WHEN YOU COMING HOME, PAPA?

By the start of 1999, my wife and I had learned that our fifth child was on the way.

That was foremost on my mind in the second full week of January as Gov. Terry Branstad gave his farewell speech to the Iowa Legislature and, three days later, incoming Gov. Tom Vilsack gave his welcoming address.

It was a strange time for me, a collision of endings and beginnings. It was particularly so as I listened to Branstad say how happy he was that he had not sought re-election. Now he said he would have more time to spend with his family.

I thought to myself, "You're going to spend more time with your kids, two of whom are adults? And here I am, with four kids ages 2 to 7 and a fifth now due in September."

I lost track of what Branstad was saying because, in my head, I couldn't stop hearing singer-songwriter Harry Chapin's classic song, "Cat's in the Cradle," and its lyrical regret about a dad too busy for his kids.

It was an epiphany to be sure, but one that had been building for a few years. I recalled a late afternoon the year before when I phoned my son, Matthieu, from the Statehouse to wish him happy birthday. He had turned 5.

And he said, "Are you coming home, Papa?" I told him that I couldn't, that I was stuck in Des Moines. "But it's my birthday," he said.

Tears started streaming down my face as I sat in the House speaker's conference room. I told my wife I would head home, but she told me to stay. She was taking the children to church camp in an hour and they wouldn't be home anyway.

This was just one of many missed moments that I regretted, and Branstad's comments about his family only reinforced what I wanted to do with my family.

My full-time job at the time was as a special projects manager at trucking firm CRST Inc. in Cedar Rapids. I called John Smith, the company's president and chief executive officer, to tell him I was thinking of stepping down from the House at the end of the 1999 session in late April.

"Are you sure you want to leave it all?" I remember him asking me.

One of my strongest supporters, Curt Hames, owner of Hames Homes in Cedar Rapids, told me to do what was best.

Always one for superlatives, Hames told me I was the greatest speaker in the history of Iowa. There can never be too many Curts, I thought.

Call what happened next good fortune or divine intervention.

Michael Blouin, the president and chief executive officer of the Cedar Rapids Area Chamber of Commerce and a former two-term U.S. representative, was stepping down from the Chamber post to accept a new job in Des Moines.

Could another politician, this time a Republican, replace him? I wondered. I quickly learned that it might be too late to ask. The Chamber's search committee had narrowed its choice to two candidates and was ready to make a pick. Nonetheless, the committee agreed to talk to me.

Committee members interviewed me on a Saturday, and as I was driving back to the Statehouse on Monday, I called the incoming Chamber board president, an insurance salesman as I had been earlier in my career, and emphasized how much I wanted to fill the Chamber's executive vacancy.

One thing I learned in the insurance business, I told him, was that you need to make the ask. You've got to try to close the sale. So I did just that.

"I would sure like the job as president of the Chamber," I said.

Five hours later, the committee members called and offered it to me.

So I walked away from it all at the Statehouse. At the time, the governor and lieutenant governor were Democrats, so as House speaker, I was the top-ranking Republican in the state. Maybe I mattered politically. Maybe I had political clout.

Just six months earlier, The Des Moines Sunday Register had given me a full-page spread on its editorial page with the headline, "Ron Corbett: ... Now House speaker, father of four, sets political sights higher. Maybe Washington."

But it was my "Cat's in the Cradle" moment. Now I had an answer to the song's recurring plea, "When you coming home, dad?" I was "papa" to my kids, and I was coming home now.

Thirteen years in one place is long enough to forget some of the details of what you did there. In the Iowa House, I had introduced, sponsored, supported, directed and roadblocked legislation, and some of it became Iowa law.

Along the way, I became a specialist of sorts because I concentrated so much on balancing the budget, controlling spending and cutting taxes.

Fundamentally, I thought of myself as a consensus builder. I think one of my strengths as House speaker and before that, as a committee chairman, was my ability to get disagreeing parties into a room to work out differences.

As for issues and accomplishments in my 13-year run, there were big ones and small ones.

We reformed the state welfare system to help recipients move into the workforce and a life of self-sufficiency.

We passed adoption reform to help prevent unfortunate legal battles like the one for Baby Jessica in the early 1990s that pitted her Iowa birth parents against adoptive parents in Michigan.

We established the Iowa Educational Savings Plan Trust, which allows parents and relatives to build tax-sheltered college accounts for those under age 17.

In addition, we created the hawk-i program—Healthy and Well Kids in Iowa—that provided health care for poor children. We provided funding to upgrade technology in public schools. We passed a law that provides state-funded special services, such as assistants for the disabled, in private schools.

I helped convene a "recreational summit" to discuss quality-of-life improvements in Iowa to help attract and keep residents. And the Restore the Outdoors initiative brought needed upgrades to Iowa's park system.

I supported the creation of the state-owned Iowa Communications Network, which has brought broadband connections across the state. But I also thought the state ought to consider privatizing the network.

I backed the state's Defense of Marriage Act, which the Iowa Supreme Court later ruled unconstitutional, as did the U.S. Supreme Court on similar federal and state laws. I also supported what I considered reasonable legislation that required doctors to notify a parent, legal guardian, grandparent, aunt or uncle at least 48 hours before performing an abortion for a minor.

I advocated for more prisons, better programming for juvenile offenders, upgrades to the facilities at the Iowa State Fair and mediation in divorce cases.

Iowa law prevented state law enforcement officers from using non-lethal options, such as bean bags and rubber bullets, unless the situation would require deadly force. We changed that law.

We approved litigation reform so golfers and golf courses couldn't be sued if an unintended, errant golf shot hit someone.

"We need to bring sanity back into our litigation system," I said at the time.

We also came to the rescue of the owner of the shoeshine stand in the Capitol after the state's General Services Administration said the owner needed $1 million worth of liability insurance to stay open.

"It was suggested that maybe we put a seat belt on the chair so nobody would fall out," I said.

In 1997, Tom Vilsack, the state senator who was running for governor, suggested that the state sell the Iowa Lottery and use the money to improve education. I called the idea "goofy" because Iowa had come to depend upon the annual revenue from the lottery to support the budget.

I also was a proponent of the Taxpayers' Rights

Amendments to the Iowa Constitution, which the Legislature approved in two different sessions, 1998 and 1999, and sent on to voters. One amendment would have required a 60 percent majority in both chambers of the Legislature to raise taxes, something opponents said would let a legislative minority control tax policy. The second amendment would have cemented into the Constitution the Iowa law that limits state spending to 99 percent of revenues.

Opponents won out. Voters rejected both amendments—52 percent to 48 percent on the 60-percent majority amendment; 51 percent to 49 percent on the 99-percent spending limit amendment.

I had been one of only two of the 100 members of the Iowa House under age 30 when I arrived in 1987.

As speaker and as someone who helped recruit candidates and campaign for them, I helped cut down on needless committee meetings, kept legislators at home in their districts on Monday morning and all day Friday and took other steps to make the place friendlier to families. It all helped us attract younger talent even if, in the end, the changes didn't keep me, at age 38.

I hadn't imagined I would stay at the Iowa Legislature for 13 years. Yet I never thought at the start of January 1999 that I would give up the speaker's job after five years and leave the House at the end of the session that April.

My new job at the Chamber of Commerce gave me a new opportunity I hadn't foreseen. And it would teach me how to take to the front-line trenches to try to make a local community better.

20

MORE THAN CUTTING RIBBONS

I was heading an organization of 1,500 member businesses, big and small, with 12 employees when I took over as president and chief executive officer of the Cedar Rapids Area Chamber of Commerce in May 1999.

My new office in downtown Cedar Rapids was peculiar, to say the least. It sat underground and had no windows. It seemed a perfect place to hide out, an invitation to embrace an us-against-them bunker mentality.

I didn't want that, and I didn't intend to let the Chamber be a stick-your-head-in-the-sand outfit. Don't get me wrong. I was eager to cut plenty of ribbons at newly opening businesses, as is the custom for Chamber officials. But we were going to engage with the community and support local projects, too.

Beyond that, I thought we also could come up with ideas and try to persuade the community to back them.

From my start at the Chamber, I realized that the Iowa Legislature, which I had just left, can affect the communities that lawmakers represent more than some might think.

It turned out that I already had set the agenda for my new job.

One of my first orders of business was to support the community's effort to secure a state Community Attraction and Tourism, or CAT, grant from a program created by the Iowa Legislature in my last session there.

Others in the Legislature and I had fought for the CAT program—to date, CAT has awarded $159 million to 427 projects in 97 of Iowa's 99 counties—because we believed our communities needed more attractions, as did Iowa, to keep and draw in more people.

In Cedar Rapids, we were among the first cities to seek a CAT grant to help replace the city's run-down, 50-year-old, minor-league baseball park. Without a new ballpark, the city feared it would lose an important summertime attraction, the city's Class A team, the Kernels.

The subsequent award of $3.2 million in CAT funds was conditional. The program required the Cedar Rapids community to come up with the rest of the money for the $14 million ballpark project. A local fundraising campaign did that, with voters agreeing to raise their city property-tax levy for four years to finish the job.

By then, I had turned my attention to another community priority—crumbling school infrastructure.

On this front, a local fracas was well underway over a proposed local-option sales tax to fund building improvements for the Cedar Rapids Community School District.

The tax proposal—other districts in the county also were seeking to pass the sales tax for their buildings—was designed to raise $148 million over 10 years to fund a long list of Cedar Rapids school projects. An advocacy group backing the school plan and an organized opposition group, Against Local Option Tax or ALOT, were going back and forth.

By October, ALOT had won out. The school district's voters soundly rejected the plan.

One thing hadn't changed. The Cedar Rapids district still needed to repair and upgrade its buildings. So, both as Chamber president and as a parent with children in school, I backed a better, scaled-back building proposal under the campaign banner "Just the Basics."

In part, the initial high-cost, sales-tax proposal failed because the Cedar Rapids Community School District had done a good job of detailing where every tax dollar would go. The long list of projects gave opponents ample opportunity to grab on to perceived extravagances to mount a case against the sales tax.

With the new proposal, we eliminated wants, focused on needs and came up with a $46 million plan that emphasized science labs, performing arts facilities and heating and cooling systems.

As part of the Support Our School campaign, which I chaired, I recruited Larry Murphy of Oelwein, Iowa, to help. I thought we could repeat the success we enjoyed working together across political party lines in the Iowa Legislature.

At one point in our effort, we stood in front of a group of school principals and took turns talking about the need to invest in our kids' futures and about the campaign to get this new building proposal approved by voters.

I said something like, "Listen, we are working hard to raise money from local businesses and individuals for the campaign. But I need all the principals to write a check out to help, too."

Then I pulled out my checkbook, Larry pulled out his, and we each wrote out checks for $250 and waved them in the air. Not many checks from principals followed.

Well. I had wanted to tell the business community that every school principal who would see the benefits from the proposed bond vote had stepped up to help. But I couldn't. Some principals gave, but I think most felt that they already were donating their lives to education.

We pushed on, building a broad coalition of supporters.

By December 2000, we took the $46 million school measure to voters as a bond issue, which is tougher to pass because, unlike a sales-tax vote, it requires approval from 60 percent of voters. One advantage of bonds is that they provide money immediately for must-do projects. A sales tax doesn't do that. It brings in money over time.

Our campaign worked. Seventy-three percent of voters approved the school plan, and it won more than 60 percent approval in each of the Cedar Rapids school district's 51 voting precincts.

Not only did the school-building effort deliver for the community, but it did for my children, too. All five have participated in show choir while in school and have used the new Washington High School performing arts facility that the bond issue put in place.

To this day, I go back to that vote in 2000 to remind myself that public officials and community leaders can ask too much from taxpayers. In that instance, Cedar Rapids voters were willing to support a reasonable request to upgrade school facilities but had not been willing to support what they saw as a lavish wish list of improvements.

Unfortunately, differentiating between wants and needs, high-cost dreams and affordable reality, never seems to get easier. Often, you don't know where the lines are until those in control of the purse strings tell you.

In early 1999, in the months before I left the Iowa Legislature, some of my legislative colleagues and I held talks with first-year Gov. Tom Vilsack about state support for bigger community attractions. At the time, proposals were circulating for a sports arena in Des Moines, a NASCAR track in Davenport and a rain forest and educational center called Iowa Child in Cedar Rapids or Des Moines.

The next year, 2000, the Legislature and Vilsack approved the creation of the Millennium Fund, which soon became the Vision Iowa program, to help bring to reality such distinctive destination projects as the National Mississippi River Museum and Aquarium in Dubuque.

Vision Iowa money over the next few years also contributed to projects in Des Moines, Council Bluffs, Davenport, Sioux City, Burlington, Waterloo and Mason City, among other places.

However, Cedar Rapids, Iowa's second-largest city, failed to obtain money from the program.

Not that the community didn't try.

At the time the Vision Iowa program started, Cedar Rapids hadn't come up with a big proposal like Dubuque's river museum that might qualify for Vision Iowa funds. For a time, some in the city had become intrigued by Des Moines businessman Ted Townsend's Iowa Child idea for an indoor rain forest and education center. But he decided to try to build the project, ultimately without success, in Coralville.

By then, Cedar Rapids had moved on to come up with its own project. From a series of community idea sessions emerged RiverRun, a riverfront redevelopment proposal. And as Chamber president, I became the community salesman for the project.

RiverRun featured a whitewater kayak course, a riverside amphitheater, a farmers market, a wetlands interpretative center, trails, fishing piers and a tow-rope ski lift to transform a soon-to-be-closed landfill affectionately called Mount Trashmore into a ski run.

However, by the time our RiverRun project made its way to the state Vision Iowa Board in January 2003, much of the $225 million in available grant money had been awarded to other cities. Cedar Rapids was seeking $25 million for RiverRun, but the Vision Iowa Board gave it much less, $10.5 million. And by design, the state award came with strings. Cedar Rapids had to come up with local matching funds to qualify for the state money.

Once again, we'd have to ask voters to pass a local-option sales tax to raise money for a project.

I headed out on the uphill climb, traveling around the city to promote RiverRun and to answer questions about it. In the process, I found myself asking voters to realize that the project would boost the sluggish local economy, create jobs and bring attractions to neglected industrial brownfield sites and an old landfill.

My assurances didn't stop the questions, some of which were about the smallest of details. What about attendance projections and the cost per user at the whitewater kayak course? Would farmers be willing to pay $2 a square foot for space in the new farmers market?

I wanted residents to see the forest, not bang into all the trees. We weren't ignoring details. But I didn't want to get bogged down in them, either.

I traveled to South Bend, Ind., with Paul Pate, who was mayor at the time, and Dan Baldwin, co-chairman of the RiverRun Committee, to see its whitewater course in action. We came away thinking our project would be better.

"RiverRun is not going to be something secondary (as the whitewater course is in South Bend) to Notre Dame football," Baldwin said at the time. "Our project is something that's going to be a premier attraction in Cedar Rapids."

It didn't turn out that way. In June 2003, voters convincingly rejected the local tax match to fund RiverRun.

Amy Johnson, the Chamber's marketing and communications director at the time, remembers that backers of the RiverRun plan knew from the start that winning voter approval would be tough, so the outcome wasn't a huge surprise.

"RiverRun was truly an idea that was way ahead of its time," Johnson says.

I was disappointed with the vote, and I took a step back.

At the same time, I realized that the defeat didn't change the fact that Cedar Rapids had been willing to look at new ideas during my first years at the Chamber.

Voters had approved tax support for a new minor-league baseball field in August 2000 and a bond issue for school upgrades in December 2000. Voters also supported money for the city's swimming pools in July 2001.

The Chamber and I supported all those community

investments.

The city eventually gave up on winning state Vision Iowa money, a decision that wasn't easy to swallow. It's a big concession for a community to turn back a multimillion-dollar state grant instead of using it to build something special.

In the years ahead, much in the concept of RiverRun came to pass as Cedar Rapids rebuilt after the city's 2008 flood. Today, there is a farmers market, called NewBo City Market, a riverfront amphitheater, the Indian Creek Nature Center's new Amazing Space facility, plans for recreational uses at the landfill site and new residential and commercial development in the RiverRun project area.

The kayak course didn't catch on in Cedar Rapids, but other courses eventually were built in Charles City, Manchester and Elkader.

As for me, nothing had changed despite the RiverRun defeat. I still wasn't going to pass up chances to improve the community. Not every deal is going to work out. But none work out if you don't try.

And I would have another two years to try before I left the Chamber.

21

RESHAPING CITY GOVERNMENT

My job at the Cedar Rapids Area Chamber of Commerce kept me close to home full time with my family. I hadn't anticipated an added benefit—a close-up view of how local government worked and didn't work.

And I had some suggestions.

The first—merging city and county government—failed to gain a following. But a second—changing and modernizing the form of Cedar Rapids city government—was a different story.

The idea of merging city and county governments was not new when I brought up the subject in 2002.

Other metro areas had merged governments, such as Louisville and Lexington, Ky., Jacksonville, Fla., Nashville, Tenn., and Kansas City, Kan.

In Iowa, too, Des Moines, Polk County and the other cities in that county voted on merging governments in 1994 and in 2004, though without success.

It seemed logical, then, that Iowa's second-largest city, Cedar Rapids, and second-largest county, Linn, ought to talk about the idea as well.

To take that question on, the Chamber commissioned a study in 2002 to examine one aspect of Cedar Rapids and Linn County governments, information technology, or IT. The study concluded that a merger of the city and county IT departments could save taxpayers almost $700,000 a year, or nearly $14 million over 20 years.

The ink was barely dry, though, before county officials said the study's numbers didn't make sense. Lumir Dostal, chairman of the Linn County Board of Supervisors at the time, added that the premise of the Chamber's study was wrong. He said Iowa didn't have too many layers of government. The more layers, the closer government got to the people, he said.

In the numbers, we at the Chamber could see only redundant government. Our research at the time showed that Iowa was seventh in the nation in number of counties—99. Only Minnesota had more than Iowa's 1,602 townships. Only three states had more city governments than Iowa's 950. And with all its jurisdictions combined, Iowa had 6 percent of the nation's governments and only 1 percent of the nation's population.

Nothing, though, came of our merger idea—at City Hall or with the county supervisors—and we set it aside.

In 2005, three years after the Chamber had shelved its merger idea, a bipartisan panel of Iowa legislators along with Gov. Tom Vilsack called for the creation of regional governments in the state to encourage cities and counties to share services. That proposal didn't go anywhere, either.

However, it did prompt us at the Chamber to dust off our 2002 study and ask Cedar Rapids and Linn County to share an information technology director. But neither thought the move would save the money we thought it would.

By that time, my focus had shifted to a second idea to improve local government.

I called Jim Cannon in the early summer of 2004 and asked him to meet me for a cup of coffee.

The 63-year-old Cannon was a private security guard who had decided in 2003 that Cedar Rapids and Linn County needed a casino. In unlikely fashion, he launched something of a one-man campaign, which in the end amassed some 12,000 signatures on petitions, forcing the county to hold a vote on gambling.

Neither I nor the Chamber of Commerce took a position on the casino referendum, which Linn County voters, including me, voted against in November 2003. Nonetheless, I admired Cannon. He reminded me that a single person or a handful of people, through hard work, could get a policy matter in front of voters.

The Chamber board of directors gave me the green light to do just that—to collect petition signatures to see if voters would consider replacing Cedar Rapids' commission government.

Only one other American city with a population of more than 100,000 people, Portland, Ore., had retained a commission government. In Cedar Rapids, it was a century-old setup that had full-time council members who doubled as commissioners and oversaw certain city departments. Most other cities long ago had turned to a government with a city manager, who was trained to run a city, and with part-time council members to set city policy.

In my view, Cedar Rapids needed a professional city manager. Our commission structure was outdated, inefficient and expensive.

Just as bad, the commission government excluded people from seeking elective office. Many good council candidates couldn't afford to give up a full-time job to become a full-time council member. In addition, the commissioner position titles—streets, parks, public safety, finance and mayor—further limited the number of people who felt qualified to run for office. As a result, career city employees often ended up as commissioners. In the City Hall election races of 2003, only seven people competed for the five jobs—five incumbents and two token candidates.

We at the Chamber also thought that the five commissioners often operated in small, colliding worlds or— fittingly, in a farm state—in their own "silos."

A perfect example was a small lake created by the Iowa Department of Transportation when it removed dirt to widen Highway 13 on the far east side of the city. Our parks commissioner promoted the spot as a fishing venue, while our finance commissioner saw it as a buffer to keep people away from the city's wastewater treatment plant next door. One commissioner was talking about crappies and bass. The other was putting up no-trespassing signs.

The petition drive that started in August quickly gathered momentum as Chamber members, local Realtors, members of a young professionals' organization and local labor unions stood with me at community events asking people to sign a petition to convene a Home Rule Charter

Commission. As set out in state law, the commission would determine which types of government organization to take to a vote.

By the end of October, we had obtained more than 10,000 signatures, about 1,000 more than needed, requiring the City Council to name a 15-member Charter Commission. On March 31, 2005, the Charter Commission voted 12-2 to ask voters to choose between two options: the city's current commission government or a government setup with a professional city manager. The council-manager option came with nine part-time council members, including a part-time mayor. Four council members would be elected citywide, including the mayor, and five would be elected in districts.

Then the battle began.

On April 5, the City Council accepted the commission's recommendation and set the vote on the two government options for June 14, 2005. It was a vote that could cost these same council members their full-time jobs if voters opted for change.

Upon setting the election date, two of the five council members, Mayor Paul Pate and Streets Commissioner Don Thomas, bashed the Chamber and, without naming names, me for working to put the change-of-government measure on the ballot.

"A political campaign is being run out of the Cedar Rapids Area Chamber of Commerce, and I think people should be aware of that," Pate said at the time. Voters, he said, had put the current council in place to build bridges, not burn them and tear the community down as the

Chamber was doing.

Thomas said the Chamber and I should spend less time meddling in city government and more time attracting businesses and helping to rejuvenate the city's downtown.

"I don't think they've been doing very well at that," Thomas said.

Mike Weston, a Cedar Rapids lawyer and chairman of the Chamber board, shot back.

"The fact of the matter is that Cedar Rapids has a top-heavy form of government with too many upper-level managers," Weston said. The Chamber's focus, he added, is to create the best business climate in the city. "Part of that is having the opportunity to serve on a citizen City Council," he said. "Soon, Cedar Rapids citizens will have an opportunity to do that."

There was no better place in Cedar Rapids to hold a news conference about city government than the lobby of the Veterans Memorial Building downtown. City Hall had been housed there ever since the building opened in 1929 on an island in the Cedar River. One wall of the lobby is a 20-foot-wide, 26-foot-tall, 9,000-piece stained-glass window, designed by artist Grant Wood to celebrate America's war veterans.

In a news conference in front of that window, Citizens to Keep the Commission mounted its campaign against the council-manager form of government.

I wasn't invited to the group's event in early May, but I wandered in, eager to listen to its "superstar"—legendary former Cedar Rapids Mayor Don Canney.

The former mayor didn't have any trouble spotting me.

He pointed a finger at me from across the lobby and mouthed the words, "You're ruining this city."

Business owner Ralph Palmer got to the microphone first and said the unelected Chamber of Commerce and its "deep pockets" wanted the city to be run by an unelected city manager.

Canney, 74 at the time, took his turn and said he didn't like city managers much. He suggested that city managers were kinglike figures whom voters couldn't replace. And he called the idea "frightening" that a city manager, not an elected official, could do nearly all the hiring in city government.

Canney and the others were pretty nasty. I was surprised how they had targeted the Chamber when many others—neighborhood leaders, young professionals and union members among them—supported the change in government as well. The members of Citizens to Keep the Commission had the chance to promote the pluses of the commission government. Instead, they were shooting the messenger, the Chamber.

A few days later, Canney and I squared off on the popular local talk-radio show at the time, "The Bob Bruce Radio Experience." Canney repeated that the Chamber and I were "wrecking the city," and I told him not to "sensationalize."

"People feel disenfranchised out there. This is a strong movement," I said. He said people would feel "disdain" for the Chamber for years to come, and I called that nonsense. I said I'd be willing to put differences aside after the June 14 vote and move ahead.

I found myself in an odd place; up against Pate, the current mayor, and Canney, a former mayor. I liked both and had worked with both.

Back in 2000, I had asked Canney to help in the successful "Just the Basics" campaign to pass a bond vote to fix school buildings. He was glad to help. He recorded a radio ad for the effort without rehearsal and in one take.

As for Pate, I still tell the story of how he drove me back to Cedar Rapids from a legislative session in Des Moines during a snowstorm when my second child was about to be born.

With Canney, our differences over the form of government did not diminish my admiration for all he had accomplished for Cedar Rapids. In 2011, I led the city effort to name the city's Eastern Iowa Airport terminal. It now is the Donald J. Canney Airport Terminal in tribute to the city's longest-serving mayor.

"He did not believe in the status quo," I said at the dedication ceremony. "He was extremely proud of Cedar Rapids. He knew that we are Iowa's second-largest city. And he wanted us to act that way."

On June 14, 2005, Cedar Rapids voters approved the change in government overwhelmingly, 68.8 percent in favor, 31.2 percent against. All 47 of the city's voting precincts passed the measure.

That November, 38 people ran for the nine new part-time council seats. It was quite a change from two years earlier, when only the five incumbents and two others had competed. Two incumbents from the full-time council competed for part-time council seats, and both were defeated.

The victory was special to me. With the support of the Chamber, I had started the change-of-government process less than a year before by launching a petition drive. Never, though, did I expect that my involvement with the new city government would continue one day in a big way.

22

A FLOOD BRINGS ME BACK
TO PUBLIC LIFE

You almost can vanish from public memory once you leave public life.

My former legislative colleague Brent Siegrist of Council Bluffs laughs to this day when he recalls what then-Iowa House member Chuck Gipp from Decorah said just after I stepped down as House speaker, resigned my legislative seat and left Des Moines in May 1999 to head the Cedar Rapids Area Chamber of Commerce.

"You know, that Larry Corbett was a hell of a speaker," Siegrist remembers Gipp saying minutes after I left the Capitol that day. Larry Corbett, not Ron Corbett. When you're gone, you're gone.

I didn't disappear, though. My new job kept me in the public spotlight, at least in Cedar Rapids, for six more years. Then, I really did sort of disappear.

In June 2005, I left the Chamber to advance my business career at trucking firm CRST Inc. I had worked there for eight years while serving in the Legislature, and now I was returning to CRST as vice president of customer service.

At the time, supporters asked me if I had an interest in running for governor in 2006. They thought my years in the

Legislature and at the Chamber would make me a good candidate, and they reminded me, too, that some had considered me gubernatorial material when I was speaker of the Iowa House in the late 1990s.

But it wasn't my time—if a person has a time. I was starting my business career anew, and my five kids were still young. Running for governor would have sent me back on the road when I wanted to stay home.

But who knew.

A historic flood hit Cedar Rapids in June 2008, and the disaster changed a lot of plans.

That month the Cedar River climbed 11 feet higher than it ever had. Floodwater covered 10 square miles of the city and damaged 6,865 residential properties, 754 commercial/industrial ones, including much of the downtown, and all of Cedar Rapids' major public buildings.

My family was high and dry as many in the city were. But too many weren't. And nearly everyone knew someone who had been hit. Among those were CRST employees, and the company, like others in the city, set up an emergency fund to help.

By early fall, some in the local business community, including my boss at CRST, John Smith, wondered what could be done to get the city's flood recovery moving more quickly and smoothly.

Smith asked me if I would consider running for mayor in 2009.

I wasn't sure. I took his suggestion to lunch with my wife and asked her what she thought. She was back in school and on to something new herself, and she told me that politics suits me, that I'm good at it and that I should run.

As for me, I had juggled a job at Equitable Life Insurance Co. and then at CRST while a part-time legislator, so I guessed I could do it again at CRST as a part-time mayor.

I had spent a combined 19 years working in the Legislature and at the Chamber to help support Cedar Rapids. I, too, thought the city was not doing enough in the important decision-making months after the flood. To its credit, the City Council was holding frequent, lengthy meetings with flood victims, so there seemed to be plenty of public input. But I was looking for more output.

So, at the end of 2008 and the start of 2009, I started trying to raise money for a mayoral campaign, knowing the two candidates had raised more than $225,000 combined in winning and losing efforts in the 2001 Cedar Rapids mayoral battle.

In early January 2009, I also conducted a phone survey to test the waters. The survey asked voters what they thought of potential mayoral candidates, including Brian Fagan, a local lawyer, City Council member and the council's mayor pro tem; council member and business owner Monica Vernon; Scott Olson, a commercial Realtor who was defeated by Kay Halloran in 2005 in a close mayoral race; and me. Halloran was not expected to seek re-election.

The results encouraged me to push forward.

Even so, the focus at City Hall and in the community at the start of 2009 was on rebuilding after the flood, not the November city elections.

Much of the work of flood recovery—renovations of flood-damaged homes, buyouts and demolitions of more than 1,000 ruined ones and decisions about the damage to the city's main public buildings—still needed to get moving.

It was clear, too, that hundreds of millions of dollars in federal disaster relief would be needed. What was less clear was if or when it might arrive. The nation had dropped into a deep recession, the solvency of the nation's banking system seemed to be in question and a new president, Barack Obama, was about to take office.

In the face of that uncertainty, Cedar Rapids decided it needed to do what it could for itself. On March 3, voters approved a 1-percent local-option sales tax for 63 months to raise about $18 million a year for Cedar Rapids flood recovery. The money would be a start, and it would come with a hope that substantial federal and state funds would follow.

Six days later, on March 9, I announced my candidacy for mayor. I did so standing in front of the flood-ruined Swiss Valley dairy processing plant and across the street from the city's flood-damaged central fire station. The dairy had decided to leave town, and the city was negotiating with the Federal Emergency Management Agency over what to do with the fire station and a long list of other flood-damaged city properties.

"Clearly, I have no doubt that Cedar Rapids' best days lie ahead," I said to an assortment of local news reporters standing in the cold. At the time, many in Cedar Rapids thought the city's best days had come and gone for good.

"The question is whether we will do this sooner rather than later," I said. "We need a new game plan that gets us moving forward and achieves the goal of sooner."

The speech is still out there on YouTube. As I've listened to it, I realize that I did acknowledge that no previous Cedar Rapids city administration had confronted the challenges that the current one was facing—of both a natural disaster and a national economic crisis at the same time.

Nonetheless, I said the city needed to speed up flood recovery, create jobs and spur economic development. It didn't need more studies, high-priced out-of-state consultants and inaction.

I called the flood-damaged fire station in front of me a "monument of delay," and I promised to replace a "culture of delay" with bold action using local talent.

Later that March, I was standing in front of the Veterans Memorial Building with a collection of unemployed local workers eager for the city to rebuild.

Just across the way, I said, the Linn County Sheriff's Office was repairing the flooded county jail and ready to move prisoners back in while the Veterans Memorial Building, home to City Hall, sat empty with no plans in place to renovate it. The city didn't need to embark on a six-month study to build a new Taj Mahal of a City Hall. It needed to return to its longtime home, I said.

Within the month, I was outside the closed Ellis Park swimming pool and the city's Tree of Five Seasons memorial, both flood-damaged without plans for repair. The city had just announced that the pool would remain closed in the flood-hit northwest Cedar Rapids neighborhoods for another year, to which I said the culture of delay had let homeowners, businesses, veterans and now the kids down. I promised to have the pool open for swimming in 2010 if elected mayor.

There were other YouTube videos easily accessible from

my campaign website. All you had to do was go to the site and click on "Corbett TV."

In one video, I talked about a five-point jobs program while I walked in a crumbling parking lot outside a closed big-box store. In another, I held up a sign about how the city was encouraging golfers to buy equipment at the city's public courses, which were exempt from collecting sales tax that was helping to fund the city's flood recovery. A third video found me standing in a mess of pigeon droppings in one city parking ramp and showed me in another ramp, which was flood-damaged and slated for demolition. I asked why it was still standing. It was another monument of delay. Bring out the dynamite, I said.

In a way, I felt like I was talking to myself. As August arrived, with the city election just three months away, no one had jumped in to challenge me. Then, on Aug. 6, City Council member Brian Fagan joined the mayoral race.

Fagan said he had been "in the trenches" of flood recovery and didn't want to walk away from all the hard work the city had done during the 14 months since the flood. He said the city needed the quality professional city management it currently had and not "professional politicians," which no doubt was an indictment of me and my 13 years in the Iowa Legislature.

He was for staying the course. I was for changing it, speeding it up.

In the eight months between the start of my campaign and the election on Nov. 3, the city had received good news. The federal government announced it would be sending the state of Iowa significant federal disaster funds for property buyouts and property renovations in Cedar Rapids and elsewhere in Iowa.

I had reason to believe that my campaign helped get the city moving, too. A week before the election, the city's flood recovery director jumped into the Ellis Park pool to declare it was repaired and would open in 2010. Maybe he had seen my YouTube video about the pool.

In the end, I defeated Fagan with 62.3 percent of the vote to his 35.7 percent. I won in 44 of the city's 47 voting precincts.

It was a margin of victory that seemed unfair to Fagan after he had worked long hours over many months on the city's flood recovery. But on election night, I disagreed with him that the city had laid the foundation for flood recovery. I said the foundation had yet to be poured.

"We've prolonged the decision-making, and because of that, people are hurting," I said.

Maybe Chuck Wieneke, a returning council member who did not face re-election in 2009, was right when he said on election night that incumbents like Fagan often take the blame in cities that are recovering from natural disasters.

"We Americans are a very impatient people," Wieneke said then. "And recovery from disaster never happens as fast as it should."

I was one of the impatient ones.

What remained unclear on election night was whether I could assemble a solid working majority on the nine-member council.

Three council members who supported me, Justin Shields, Monica Vernon and Chuck Swore, would be on the new council, but a fourth dependable vote was still up in the air.

That changed in December in a runoff for two of the council seats. Don Karr Jr., who also supported me, won one of the seats. In the other runoff, the candidate who supported me lost.

It looked like I might have a 5-4 working majority when the new council took office in January.

23

MY FIRST 100 DAYS
AS MAYOR

It took two months, between my election victory on Nov. 3 and my swearing in as mayor on Jan. 2, 2010, to get to my first 100 days in office.

Those two transition months were active ones. Had the central theme of my mayoral campaign—replace a culture of delay with one of action—made an impact?

Within a week of the election, the state of Iowa announced that it would send Cedar Rapids $95.5 million of U.S. Department of Housing and Urban Development funds to buy out a group of 892 flood-damaged properties. These numbers would grow in the months and years ahead. The money was in addition to $7.4 million that had been released by the Federal Emergency Management Agency to buy out 100 or so of the most flood-prone properties closest to the Cedar River.

On Dec. 3, the city announced it had mailed out the first 55 property buyout offers to flood victims, though the first three of what would become 1,356 property buyouts would not be completed until the end of February, 20 months after the city's June 2008 flood.

Then on Dec. 16, a developer moved dirt for the first of

numerous new multifamily housing complexes to be built over the next five years with private and public funds to replace affordable housing lost in the flood and more.

To be fair, the spurt of post-election, flood-recovery activity showed that city, state and federal officials had worked hard the previous 18 months to move through what was surely a bureaucratic swampland of regulations. Holdovers from the previous council, including Monica Vernon, Justin Shields and Tom Podzimek, have not been shy about reminding me of this.

Vernon says the previous council established the under-pinnings of recovery. It's like that phoenix rising. You don't see it at first. It's down in the ashes. It began to emerge as I did as the new mayor, she says.

For my part, I had campaigned for nearly a year press-ing the city to get moving. Now, I was eager to work with the new council and was happy to see results.

On the Saturday morning after the election, I met with the Cedar Rapids city manager, Jim Prosser, at a local restaurant, the Spring House. The name fit with my plate of fresh ideas.

The meeting, though, wasn't without some chilliness. After all, my mayoral campaign had criticized—well, city man-agement. I had complained about a lack of speed and results on flood recovery, the use of out-of-state consultants and the plan to build what I thought was a new, unneeded City Hall.

Over breakfast, Prosser handed me a thick document, which outlined the "balanced decision-making" approach to city management that he had championed in his three-plus years as city manager. But I was less interested in the process, in the sausage making, and more in results. I wanted to see meat on the plate.

In that spirit, I spelled out my priorities. We had to decide immediately on what to do with key, flood-damaged city properties—the library, central fire station and City Hall. We had to accelerate the pace of buyouts for home-owners. We had to devise a plan to spend revenue from the eight-month-old local-option sales tax for flood-recovery projects. And we had to adopt a buy-local policy.

My strong opposition to one issue—building a $38 million City Hall—apparently hadn't mattered much. City officials, the lame-duck City Council and their consultants held post-election public open houses in mid-November to discuss options, which included the new building.

In the process, some 150 people, including 40 city staff members, filled out comment cards, and the largest number, 56, backed the idea of a new city hall. A new city hall appeared to be the preferred option for how to proceed. With such a small sample, the math didn't add up to me.

On Jan. 2, I made a point to hold the swearing-in ceremony for the new City Council in the lobby of the flood-damaged and still-closed Veterans Memorial Building, which had housed City Hall until the flood. The lobby, with its towering, Grant Wood-designed, stained-glass window, was the perfect place for me to say in my first official remarks that the city wasn't going to build a new City Hall if I had my way. And by then, I was all but sure I had the votes on the new council to back me.

I said I felt I had been elected to pick up the pace of flood recovery and to push for an economic development agenda that would lift the city out of its part of a deep national recession.

We began to do both.

In 100 days, my council colleagues and I decided where to build the new $45 million library by a razor-thin vote; discarded the idea of building a new City Hall; and signaled an interest in moving City Hall from the Veterans Memorial Building to the empty, now-city-owned, former federal courthouse just down the street.

We also made the first property buyout purchases; won permission to pay 107 percent of each property's pre-flood assessed value; and made sure that certain earlier flood-relief payments did not count against the buyout amounts.

In addition, we ended the contract of a highly paid consultant. And we agreed to take on debt to build a new convention center and remodel the event arena next to it so we didn't lose a $35 million federal grant and $15 million state grant for the project.

And on April 12, my 101st day in office, Prosser resigned his city manager post, and the City Council approved a separation agreement with him.

Dan Baldwin, who was head of the Greater Cedar Rapids Community Foundation at the time, was among a group of community leaders who hustled to Grand Forks, N.D., to see how it had recovered from its 1997 flood disaster even as floodwaters still were receding in Cedar Rapids in June 2008. Most of Grand Forks' elected officials were not returned to office in the first election after the flood, Grand Forks officials told him.

"Given the circumstances and the nature of the decisions that had to be made—Cedar Rapids' was a disaster on a scale that no city in the state ever had to deal with—maybe the same (result for elected officials) is true with the city manager," Baldwin said then of Prosser's departure. "... It was almost a given, at a certain juncture, it was going to lead to this."

The ongoing challenges of flood recovery helped to keep my ego in check.

In the minutes before I took the oath as mayor in the Veterans Memorial Building, I toured the spacious third-floor mayor's office with windows looking out to the river and the downtown. That office would never be mine.

For my first few years as mayor, I shared a couple of cubicles with the other council members in a northeast Cedar Rapids office building that became the temporary city hall after the 2008 flood. Until June 2014, when City Hall moved back downtown into the former federal court-house, my office for all practical purposes was my car.

Once I became mayor, I established a five-vote nucleus or working majority on the nine-member council, but I didn't get my way on every council vote, and some votes were hardly unanimous.

In those first 100 days, I did succeed in pushing for a council vote on the new library. My interest was getting it to a vote, not getting my way on where to build it. And that was a good thing. I favored a library site a short distance from downtown only to lose out when the council majority picked a better positioned, but more expensive, downtown site across Greene Square from the Cedar Rapids Museum of Art. Nothing was lost. The less expensive site I favored for the library became the home of the new central fire station.

I was particularly insistent that the city do as much as

it could as fast as it could for the 1,350 or so property owners who qualified for a property buyout now that federal money had arrived.

For instance, I did not like that we were prepared to pay owners 100 percent of the pre-flood assessed value of their properties when Waterloo won state and federal approval to pay 120 percent and Iowa City, 112 percent. I wanted to seek state permission to pay 110 percent, but was voted down by the council. Then I asked the city assessor to look at the numbers. He determined that 107 percent of pre-flood assessed value was equal to the true market value, and that's what the council and the state approved.

We also agreed to use some of the revenue from the city's local-option sales tax for flood recovery—which we had yet to spend—for two purposes: to pay for required environmental assessments of buyout properties; and to cover costs so 400 or so homeowners, who typically received up to $25,000 toward a replacement home, didn't have that earlier benefit deducted from the buyout amount.

On Feb. 20, the city closed on the first three home buyouts.

"Having to wait, it's been a cloud hanging over us since the flood," one of the three property owners, Stacy Michalec, said at the time.

With the buyouts now coming, and at 107 percent of value, I hoped the flood victims felt like we were fighting for them.

I'd be lying if I said flood recovery never seemed over-whelming. I credit my time at Cornell College in Mount Vernon, which features a one-course-at-a-time method of study, with helping to get me through.

We concentrated on buyouts for a few weeks, next on the library, then on City Hall, and on and on. And like at Cornell, we were going to complete the assignment at hand whether we liked the professor, the subject matter or the kids in the class.

My first 100 days as mayor taught me, too, that achieving the city's goals would require maneuvering through a daunting bureaucracy. That meant countless meetings, negotiations, appeals and trips to Des Moines and Washington, D.C.

There the debates centered on interpretations of federal and state rules, the size of disaster payments and how to get flood protection. We met and met with state agencies and with the Federal Emergency Management Agency, the Department of Housing and Urban Development, the Army Corps of Engineers and Iowa's congressional members and their staffers.

It's easy to beat up on the bureaucracy. The very word signifies a negative. It's all about safeguards, I'm told.

No one knows better than my City Council colleagues and me that our successes over the years of flood recovery would not have come without the long hours and competence of the city's professional staff, Iowa state officials, federal officials and Iowa's congressional delegation.

Flood recovery continued in Cedar Rapids for more than six years after I took office as mayor. Among the last steps of the recovery came on Dec. 29, 2014, when the city closed on the last of 1,356 property buyouts—the Smulekoff's Home Store along the river in downtown.

In August 2016, the city dedicated its final flood-recovery building project, the new Northwest Recreation Center.

24

HAVE CALCULATOR,
WILL TRAVEL

I was vice president for human resources at trucking firm CRST when I was elected to the part-time post of Cedar Rapids mayor in 2009.

The company stressed to all its executives and managers the importance of controlling costs, and it produced daily spreadsheets that tracked every kind of expense—number of loads, revenue per truck mile, average length of haul, miles traveled between loads, and on and on.

To drive home the point, the company handed out large desk calculators to each of us. The message from Dave Rusch, CRST president and chief executive officer, was simple: Use it.

As newly elected mayor, I packed the clunky calculator into a briefcase as I moved between my full-time job at CRST and my part-time one as mayor at City Hall.

I never imagined how much I'd use that machine for city business. And as a plus, it doubled nicely as a desk ornament and a message that I was not a tax-and-spender.

The start of any new year requires city councils in Iowa to develop a new city budget and finalize it by March 15 for the new fiscal year that begins July 1.

That first city budget deliberation proved to be a bumpy ride.

I immediately found myself at odds with our city manager and some council veterans, who wanted to raise the city's tax levy to, in part, fix the city's long-neglected streets.

My council colleague Chuck Wieneke described his thinking perfectly when he said, "I'm ashamed to drive down the street."

Another council veteran, Tom Podzimek, said the council needed to stay disciplined and committed to its long-range plan, which had been adopted before I arrived on the council and called for investment in the city's crumbling infrastructure.

I disagreed. I saw the call for an increase in the tax levy as more growth in government. I thought we could fund a few priority street projects and put off raising taxes and taking on more debt. I thought, too, that there were places in the proposed budget to save money—by not filling job vacancies for six months, for instance, or by getting rid of extras like the city newsletter.

"I'm not asking for a moonshot. I'm not asking for a miracle," I told my council colleagues.

The budget battle went on during a series of long evening sessions in which the council reviewed, line by line, each city department's budget. For each session, I had my trusty desk calculator out, tapping in numbers and tallying the savings as items dropped out of the budget.

In the end, the council voted, 5-4, to approve a new budget without a tax levy increase.

I simply could not vote for a levy increase when the nation was in the middle of the deepest recession since the Great Depression and the city was still in the early stages of recovering from the flood disaster of 2008.

At the time, too, business owners and residents who had lost their properties in the flood were leaving town. It wasn't time to raise the tax rate and encourage others to move away.

Council member Kris Gulick, who was among the four "no" votes on the budget plan, objected to the use of $1.8 million from the city's cash reserves to balance the $95 million, property-tax-supported general fund budget.

Gulick, an accountant and business consultant, called it "deficit spending" and said dipping into reserves was a practice frowned on by credit-rating agencies.

I asked him if the council had called it "overtaxing" during the years the city built up its reserve fund to equal 32 percent of the general fund budget. This one-time use of cash reserves would leave the reserve fund at 31 percent, still well above the city's directive to keep it at a minimum of 25 percent.

"If ever in the history of our community it was time to dip into the 'rainy-day fund,' this would be it," I said.

In the end, at the close of the budget year 15 months later, the city hadn't needed to use reserve funds after all.

It's fair to say that the city budget process didn't get any easier over the years.

Costs for cities, like for its residents, go up every year, and Cedar Rapids has had costs for flood recovery that most cities don't face.

In my first seven years as mayor, the City Council held the city's property-tax levy at the same level, $15.216 per $1,000 of taxable valuation.

It's the lowest levy rate among Iowa's six largest cities.

In truth, we've taken in more property-tax revenue even with an unchanged levy rate because property values have increased and a state formula has allowed more of the value of residential property to be taxed.

In recent years, too, the council has approved a franchise fee on the use of electricity and natural gas in the city rather than raise the property-tax levy. One advantage of a franchise fee is that exempt properties not subject to property taxes, such as hospitals, also pay the fee and contribute to the cost of running the city.

In that first budget fight in 2010, my council colleagues Wieneke and Podzimek were correct when they said the city had a crumbling infrastructure that needed significant attention and spending. I just didn't think we could afford it that year and I thought we should look for a revenue source other than property taxes to pay for it.

In May 2011, the City Council did not impose a new tax, but instead asked voters if they wanted to extend the city's 1 percent local-option sales tax, or LOST, to pay for flood protection and to fix streets. They didn't.

We asked again in March 2012 if they wanted to extend the local-option sales tax just for flood protection. They said no again.

Then in November 2013, voters said yes. They agreed to extend the local-option sales tax—which already was in place until June 30, 2014, for flood recovery projects—for 10 years to fix streets. The revenue now is funding a program the city calls Paving for Progress.

That's one benefit of a local-option sales tax: Voters decide.

Nearly all of Iowa's 900 or so cities and towns and 97 of

its 99 counties have a LOST in place.

Another LOST benefit is that those who don't live in a city, but shop and spend money there, also pay the local sales tax in that city. So in Cedar Rapids, they contribute, as do the residents, to repair the streets they use.

I left CRST in 2015 to work full time on Engage Iowa, a conservative think tank I created to address issues on the economy, education and the environment.

CRST let me keep the company calculator.

25

A GOVERNOR, A MAYOR AND LABOR

Who would have guessed that a testy dispute over labor unions would erupt in late 2010 between two career Republicans—Iowa's next governor and me—as my first year as Cedar Rapids mayor was coming to an end.

After all, Terry Branstad and I are both Republicans of a similar sort. Call it common-sense conservative. Or Sen. Chuck Grassley Republican.

Furthermore, Branstad and I had worked together and generally gotten along for years in the 1980s and 1990s. He was in his first stretch as governor then, and I had worked my way up to be selected by my Republican colleagues as speaker of the Iowa House of Representatives.

And for goodness' sake, in October 2010, he took time from his gubernatorial campaign to call me on my 50th birthday.

I guess the brouhaha that was to come started with that phone call.

Once the call ended, I suppose he realized that I—still in my first year in the non-partisan job of Cedar Rapids mayor—couldn't endorse him for governor as I had every time he had run for the office in the past. As for me, it was sinking in how different state government is from local government in Iowa.

City governments in Iowa are, by law, non-partisan, so party affiliation defined me much less as mayor than it did in my legislative days.

Still, I've never forgotten which team I'm on. The Republican team. But I also have enjoyed the non-partisan world, where some of my City Council colleagues have been Democrats, some Republicans and some—I just haven't known what they are.

In a broader sense, I've never thought of myself as an unbending ideologue. Even in my time in the Legislature, I like to think I worked well across the political-party divide.

To remind myself of that, I've kept a 1993 political cartoon by Brian Duffy of The Des Moines Register that shows one of my legs tied to one of the legs of Sen. Larry Murphy, a Democrat from Oelwein, Iowa, as the two of us are making our way forward. The column that accompanied the cartoon, by Register political columnist David Yepsen, said Murphy and I—we both chaired the Appropriation Committees in our respective legislative chambers—had created a "refreshing" alliance. We had replaced political dogma and gridlock with pragmatism and results, Yepsen wrote.

In 2010, my first year as Cedar Rapids mayor, the pace of the city's recovery from its devastating flood of June 2008 was accelerating, in no small part because an infusion of federal and state disaster dollars began to arrive.

Much of the state money came via the new I-JOBS program, an infrastructure investment initiative that Gov. Chet Culver, a Democrat, designed with two goals in mind: to stimulate the state economy at a time of a deep national recession; and to help Iowa communities recover from flooding and other natural disasters.

The list of Cedar Rapids recovery projects that won I-JOBS support is long. The state grants helped the city fill funding gaps so it could build a library, central fire station, district fire station, public works facility, convention center and riverfront amphitheater. The money also made it possible to renovate the city's Paramount Theatre, City Hall and the Veterans Memorial Building.

So it was hard for me to ignore how Culver's I-JOBS program was delivering vital investment to Cedar Rapids' post-disaster rebuilding effort even as his opponent, Branstad, was out on the campaign trail beating up on I-JOBS, calling it big-government spending.

For his part, Branstad said he was willing to help Cedar Rapids in its flood recovery, but he didn't think the state should be taking on debt to do so. He had a point. I-JOBS wasn't without its flaws. At the local level, though, I was just happy that Cedar Rapids was getting the state support it so vitally needed.

If elected, I knew that Branstad couldn't do anything about Culver's signature jobs program. But I knew, too, there might be a problem with a second Culver initiative— his executive order to permit project labor agreements on state-funded building projects.

My City Council colleagues and I were contemplating the use of just such a labor agreement even as candidate Branstad was vowing to scrap such deals if elected. In fact, he had made his disdain for the labor agreements clear in a debate with Culver at Coe College in Cedar Rapids a month before the November vote. I was sitting in one of the first few rows of the auditorium that night. I heard him clearly.

Branstad easily defeated Culver, with 52.3 percent of the votes to the incumbent's 42.8 percent, an outcome that would soon leave me in a quandary.

Here I was, a lifelong Republican, in negotiations as Cedar Rapids' non-partisan mayor with the local building trades unions, which lean toward Democrats, on a project labor agreement that the incoming Republican governor detested.

My political life had started out simpler.

Back in 1986, in my first run for the Iowa Legislature, I defeated local labor leader and incumbent lawmaker Doris Peick, a Democrat. Local labor didn't like me much.

Early on as a legislator, though, I made a point of attending regular monthly meetings of the Hawkeye Labor Council just as I went to Chamber of Commerce meetings and meetings sponsored by the League of Women Voters. The Labor Council didn't see many Republicans at its events.

I figured that labor represented people, and, as an Iowa lawmaker, I should be listening to a lot of people, not just some. And I wanted to hear what union members had to say. For all I knew, I might need their votes.

Justin Shields, a City Council colleague of mine who was president of the Hawkeye Labor Council when I was in the Legislature, reminds me to this day that he had plenty of skepticism when I showed up back then.

He says I'd attend labor meetings on Saturdays and vote against labor on Mondays in the Legislature. Over time, he says he came to credit me for, if nothing else, being there on Saturdays.

In May 1999, I left the Legislature as speaker of the House

to head the Cedar Rapids Area Chamber of Commerce.

My Chamber agenda didn't call for much partisanship. I wanted to see the community build a minor-league ballpark, pass a school bond issue, push for support of a riverfront redevelopment project and change the shape of local government. To do that, I needed to build a coalition of people and groups of every kind. I asked labor union members, among many others, to help, and they did.

Cooperation was particularly necessary in January 2010, when I took office as Cedar Rapids mayor. My City Council colleagues and I found ourselves in a once-in-a-lifetime, post-disaster, city rebuilding effort. It was an enormous task, and it only made sense for me to draw on the coalition that had helped me at the Chamber of Commerce. That coalition included the local building trades unions.

For us on the council, we very much wanted local workers and local companies to do as much of the city's rebuilding as possible. Our struggling local economy needed that type of jolt.

It was those local economic interests that persuaded us to look at the idea of a project labor agreement for our biggest building project, the city's new convention center, which was partially funded with state I-JOBS money.

We weren't alone in thinking about a labor agreement. Locally, the Linn County Board of Supervisors praised the agreement it had in place to build the county's Juvenile Justice Center. Similar labor agreements also were being planned for two upcoming state projects, a new University of Iowa Health Care clinic in Coralville and the expansion of the Iowa Veterans Home in Marshalltown.

Even so, we knew that the labor agreements were political hot potatoes. Many Republicans shared Branstad's feelings, saying the agreements drive up costs and restrict the number of contractors willing to bid on projects. In turn, many Democrats say the agreements help employ local workers in safe conditions with good wages and benefits and come with the prohibition against strikes.

For me, I hadn't given project labor agreements much thought.

That's when Ray Dochterman, who then was business manager of the local Plumbers and Pipefitters union, asked me if I had ever read such an agreement. I hadn't. I only knew the opinions.

As I read the agreement under consideration by the city, I found it to be different from what I thought it would be. It read like a community workforce agreement that would help ensure local workers did the local work.

On Nov. 9, a week after Branstad defeated Culver in the governor's race, my council colleagues and I agreed to pursue an agreement with the Cedar Rapids/Iowa City Building Trades Council for work on the city's new convention center.

On Dec. 14, the City Council voted to sign the agreement on a 7-2 vote.

The "no" votes came from Tom Podzimek and Pat Shey, both construction contractors at the time, who said the agreement with labor would prevent some workers from having a chance to be hired for the project.

Voting with the council majority, Kris Gulick, an accountant and business consultant, said the agreement would help ensure that a big, out-of-state contractor wouldn't use only out-of-state workers on the project. Another "yes" vote came from Chuck Wieneke, a former

Republican candidate for the Iowa Legislature, who said the labor agreement wouldn't affect the project cost because federal money being used on the project would require "prevailing" wages, which typically are union wages. The labor agreement would assure local workers would be used, he said.

On Jan. 14, 2011, one month to the day after the city of Cedar Rapids agreed to sign the project agreement with the local building trades council, Gov. Branstad was sworn into office. And he delivered on his campaign promise. Among his first acts on that first day was to issue Executive Order 69, which banned project labor agreements on projects using state funds.

It made me think about another campaign promise— my own for mayor in 2009—when I pledged to buy local, build local, employ local.

With Branstad's action, my council colleagues and I decided not to panic. We thought our $15 million I-JOBS grant on the $75 million convention center project was safe because we had put our labor agreement in place before the governor's new ban.

He disagreed, and he controlled the state funds.

"The governor carries a big stick, and nobody wants to get whacked by it," I said at the time as the dispute between us heated up.

By early March, I offered two proposals to reach a compromise. One called for the city to use state I-JOBS funds on parts of the convention center project other than actual construction contracts, such as land acquisition, furniture and professional services. The second idea asked the state to shift the I-JOBS grant to other city building projects, such as the central fire station and the library, which did not have labor agreements in place.

I was trying to resolve the dispute, keep the governor happy and use local labor.

The next day, Branstad visited the Cedar Rapids metro area and made it clear he was not budging.

"They knew (the ban) was coming because right in the debate (with Culver) in Cedar Rapids (in October)—and everybody who was there knows how emphatically I stated it—I said that I think project labor agreements are wrong and that I intended to reverse that. They were on notice of that," the governor said.

For a brief time, my council colleagues and I contemplated taking the fight with the governor to court, but we didn't. The city needed a convention center, and we couldn't risk losing the $15 million state grant or the $35 million federal disaster grant for the project.

Instead, the city and the Cedar Rapids/Iowa City Building Trades Council agreed to tear up the agreement on the convention center project, and the state released the project's I-JOBS funds. Cedar Rapids signed a new agreement with the local trades council on two other projects, neither of which had state funding.

In the end, I didn't consider the Branstad victory a defeat for the city.

Yes, I fought the governor on the labor agreement. The governor took a partisan position on it, and I took a rebuilding-the-city position. From my view, Cedar Rapids residents suffered in the flood, and I wanted them to have the chance to participate in the rebuilding.

You build coalitions to get things done. To have accomplishments, it's only logical to reach out to as many people as you can. For us in Cedar Rapids, that included the building trades unions.

If you think about it, it's not any different than the coalition that President Ronald Reagan is credited with creating when he won the backing of some union Democrats. In fact, Republicans still fondly reminisce about the Reagan Democrats and how wonderful it was that Reagan reached into the labor movement for support.

In 2016, Donald Trump, who is credited with getting votes from some union households, did it too. Trump defeated Hillary Clinton in Iowa by 9.3 percentage points.

Trump talks about the forgotten men and women. And in rebuilding Cedar Rapids, I wanted to make sure we didn't forget the local carpenter, plumber, pipefitter, electrician, ironworker, truck driver, bulldozer operator and all the rest.

If Republicans are red and Democrats blue, in my own way I broke down some of the blue walls in Cedar Rapids.

At the local level, we came to see that political labels don't always matter so much. Take the labels off, and you just have people who want better schools, a more efficient local government and a rebuilt city. Why wouldn't individuals and groups of every kind—Republicans, Democrats, independents, businesses, schools, churches, non-profit groups and, yes, labor—be a part of all that?

26

OPEN FOR BUSINESS

I got my first hint of how wonderful a job and an income can be on Friday evenings growing up, when my mom and dad cashed their weekly paychecks and my mom took my sisters and me grocery shopping and to McDonald's.

In our own simple way, my classmates and I joined the American economy in 1978 when our Junior Achievement team at Newton High School came up with the idea to produce "Red Pride" bumper stickers and sell them for $1 each to supporters of our playoff-bound, high school football team. It seemed every vehicle in town displayed one.

Our business venture helped give us a sense of worth, and I think it made Newton feel good as a community and optimistic about the future.

I hope in my time in the public eye that I've never lost sight of the obvious: Supporting business to help it blossom matters a lot.

Over the years, too, I've seen how competition for businesses has grown tougher and major economic development victories more elusive.

States continue to fight one another to attract companies as they work to keep their own companies from leaving.

But what has surprised me most as mayor of Cedar Rapids is the spirited rivalry between neighboring cities. It may be today's toughest battleground for jobs.

In 1999, when I left the Iowa Legislature to head the Cedar Rapids Area Chamber of Commerce, Cedar Rapids was still living off the legend of its longest-serving mayor, Don Canney. He had a knack for helping to bring manufacturing plants to the city during his 22-plus years in office. But people had lost sight of the fact that Canney retired from city government in 1992.

By the start of the new millennium, Canney-era victories were fewer and farther between. Companies were consolidating, not expanding, and some were moving to the South or outside the United States in pursuit of lower costs.

Cedar Rapids had done well by the old economic model. We set aside land for local industrial parks; we promoted the city with a toll-free 800 number; and we embraced the development chant of "recruit, recruit, recruit." No less noticeable, though, were the manufacturing plants that left town. By the early 2000s, the model had run out of gas.

In its place came the idea of "grow your own." Instead of recruiting trips, a community's economic development officials were paying more attention to existing companies, encouraging them to stay and expand. There was a new effort as well to help local entrepreneurs turn ideas into new companies and new jobs.

The perplexing questions, though, stayed the same: Why do companies stay or go, expand or stagnate, move to your city or somewhere else?

One official duty of the Cedar Rapids mayor, which is written into the 2005 City Charter, is to lead the economic development effort at City Hall. This role has taught me that a city can shape its own future even if some things end up out of its control.

From the start, my City Council colleagues and I have emphasized that Cedar Rapids is "open for business." If the city had a reputation of being unfriendly to business, that was going to end. Instead of saying "No, we can't do that," we were going to say, "Let's try to find a solution for that."

To show we were serious, we hired City Manager Jeff Pomeranz away from West Des Moines, where he had overseen a level of growth and development nearly unrivaled elsewhere in Iowa. We wanted to bring that savvy to Cedar Rapids at a crucial time, 2010, as the city continued to recover from its flood disaster of 2008.

Pomeranz helped us roll out the red carpet for business prospects while keeping an eye on bordering cities that can use tax incentives to lure Cedar Rapids businesses to move next door.

In any one year, losing a company to a neighboring city might not mean much, but it can matter a lot over a decade if you aren't paying attention.

Understand, I'm not opposed to the idea of regional economic development. A victory for one city in a metro area can be good for all the other cities. An employee might work in a neighboring city, but live, shop and pay taxes in your city. I realize that. After all, I was president and chief executive officer from 1999 to 2005 of the Cedar Rapids "Area" Chamber of Commerce.

Nonetheless, as mayor of Cedar Rapids, I've wanted to make sure businesses weren't being enticed away. If there was any enticing, I wanted us to do it, both to keep employers and to attract new ones.

Defending turf and working to attract businesses often involves incentives. It is a fact of life.

I quickly was reminded of that as I was about to take office. Physicians' Clinic of Iowa (PCI) announced in 2009 that it would move from its existing Cedar Rapids location and build a $40 million-plus regional medical clinic, possibly next door in Hiawatha.

Keeping PCI in the city was especially important because the proposed Cedar Rapids site for the new building sat between the two hospitals in the heart of the city's new medical district. We wanted to strengthen the district with the clinic development, not hurt the new district by losing PCI.

However, the city's incentive package for the project touched a nerve when the City Council agreed, on a split vote, to accede to the clinic's request and close two blocks of Second Avenue SE, a major arterial street into downtown. The clinic's doctors wanted part of the new PCI building to sit on the street as well as on both sides of it.

Council member Tom Podzimek said closing the street would help define the city's new medical district and add "vibrancy" to it. He said Second Avenue SE, the wide thoroughfare that served the downtown in the days when it was a retail powerhouse, had become an idle "runway" much of the day.

Council member Monica Vernon, though, said the city should require PCI to build over the street rather than take a significant piece of the city's transportation system out of commission.

I voted with the majority in October 2010 to close the street. The vote was 6-3. I agreed with council members Pat Shey and Kris Gulick that PCI's project was a "game-changer" for the city and for our new medical district. The clinic since has expanded and exceeded its job-creation goals.

But that hasn't been the final word. Decisions like this one stick around. Even today, residents stop me in the grocery store and at community events to tell me that we got it wrong.

My most publicized fight for jobs in the Cedar Rapids metro area also came in 2010, six months into my term as mayor, when Cedar Rapids and Hiawatha competed to land GoDaddy, the Internet company known for its flashy TV ads.

Maybe Danica Patrick, the glamorous race car driver in GoDaddy's lime-green and black corporate colors at the time, raised the dispute's profile into more than it was.

In the dustup, Hiawatha took exception to my last-minute "Hail Mary" effort to persuade GoDaddy to change its plans and move to downtown Cedar Rapids to help with the city's flood recovery. From Hiawatha's perspective, it seemed like big bully Cedar Rapids was trying to steal jobs from its smaller neighbor. Lost in the hullabaloo was the fact that GoDaddy had occupied a small office in Cedar Rapids before it announced it would close that office and expand to Hiawatha. It was my thought that Cedar Rapids was the one getting robbed.

We didn't win that one, but I didn't lose heart.

The GoDaddy battle motivated us in Cedar Rapids to

reach out to employers so we'd know about a company's plans and what intercity battles might be looming.

And the potential battles are constant, weekly.

In the wake of the GoDaddy matter, I think Hiawatha Mayor Tom Theis had it right when he said he wasn't going door to door in Cedar Rapids trying to steal businesses. Or as he put it: "I'm not a scavenger for the city of Hiawatha. If they call, I talk."

In Cedar Rapids, we wanted to make the calls to Cedar Rapids employers so they wouldn't have to call Hiawatha or anyone else.

In 2017, Cedar Rapids still is out there vying for what I call the whales; the big new plants or technology complexes that cities continue to dream about and compete for. There is a new 1,300-acre industrial park near the city's Eastern Iowa Airport just waiting for a big catch.

Even so, the financial incentives offered by some states and metro areas for the biggest projects often are out of reach for Iowa and many of its metro areas.

But there are fish to catch.

To do so, Cedar Rapids and cities across Iowa rely on a similar bait: a local property-tax incentive called tax-increment financing, or TIF.

The TIF incentive is often misunderstood and can be a target for critics who say TIFs are unfair tax breaks for business and City Hall giveaways. TIF is neither if used reasonably. TIF is just a piece of the open-for-business tool kit.

With a TIF, a community forgoes property-tax revenue for a period of years in trade, so to speak, for a business' willingness to build a project. A five-year or 10-year waiver of property taxes ends before you know it. Then, the new development is taxed on its full property value for decades to come.

In the last couple of years, my City Council colleagues and I have approved incentives for companies willing to invest in the downtown and urban renewal areas and for those that provide high-quality jobs, restore brownfield sites and preserve historic buildings. The city is open for business. It's not an open checkbook. The incentives come with a guarantee of a public benefit.

For us at City Hall, we want to encourage investment. We want new buildings to go up. We want more jobs. We want to grow and progress.

I still get asked all the time when I'm going to do something to land the whale, the major new employer, for Cedar Rapids. "But what about Apache Hose?" I ask people. "What about its $7 million expansion?"

Apache Hose, a home-grown Cedar Rapids manufacturing company, was looking to expand in 2015 and to invest either at its site in Cedar Rapids or a location out of state. It was late afternoon on Thanksgiving Eve, and City Manager Jeff Pomeranz and I were at the plant, going back and forth, selling Cedar Rapids and trying to finalize the deal. The Apache Hose executives had done their homework. They had pluses and minuses for each choice. We sweetened the city's incentive a bit and shook hands.

"Well, that's nice. But what new company do you have moving to town?" people still ask.

27

TAKING ON URBAN EYESORES

We bought a hotel. And my Cedar Rapids City Council colleagues and I didn't stop there.

After the purchase of the bankrupt hotel in early 2011 at a bargain-basement cost of $3.2 million, we renovated the 16-story, 267-room lifeblood of Cedar Rapids' downtown for about $45 million. Now we own it. Hilton Hotels runs it for us as a DoubleTree by Hilton. And we use our share of the profit to pay off the debt.

Trust me, this hasn't been easy to explain to everyone. I, a free-market Republican, have trouble believing it.

I can say this, too: Having spent 13 years in state government and seven years as Cedar Rapids mayor, no layer of government is closer to the people who elect you or closer to the firing line of citizen dismay than local government.

Sometimes it seems you lose votes with every decision you make. You can get some of them back. But yes, I still hear a lot about the hotel.

The writing had been on the wall for years for the city's only remaining downtown hotel, which opened in 1979.

The hotel had operated under the Crowne Plaza flag, and it was sold in 2007 with the understanding that the new owners would lose the Crowne Plaza name and the status that goes with it if they did not invest millions to make required upgrades to the property.

The required level of investment never came. By December 2009, creditors bought the hotel at a sheriff's sale and went on the hunt for a new owner. They didn't find one. By February 2011, the hotel closed, and the city finalized its purchase the next month.

The city's acquisition brought risk, but opportunity as well.

I looked at it this way: People nationwide had become disenchanted with Washington, D.C., and even with state legislatures and their inability to break through partisan gridlock to get something done. In contrast, I think my council colleagues and I have been willing to muscle in to solve problems when it might have been easier to stay out.

We agreed on this: Cities don't want to stand still. Standing still is a front-row ticket to decline.

At the time we purchased the hotel, the city was still hard at work trying to recover from the flood of 2008.

As part of the recovery, we were preparing to build a convention center and to renovate the city's entertainment arena next to it with the help of a $35 million federal disaster grant and a $15 million state I-JOBS grant. Not bringing the failing hotel, which would be connected to both event facilities, into the modern era would have been like remodeling your kitchen with new cabinets and countertops and leaving broken-down appliances in place.

If not for the city's intervention, the hotel most likely would have become an empty eyesore, a menacing memorial to urban decay.

Some eyesores in a community stick around so long that people who pass them every day stop seeing them. But visitors notice. As for an abandoned hotel in the heart of downtown, it always would be a jarring sight for everyone. You'd never stop thinking: How did it come to this? Who were the community leaders who let this happen?

In buying the hotel, we took comfort in knowing that Cedar Rapids wasn't alone. Other cities across the country had ventured into hotel ownership, too, to prevent urban blight and to bolster the prospects of a downtown, a convention center, or both. This wasn't uncharted territory.

Remember, too, it was 2011. The city and the nation were still trying to climb out of a severe economic downturn. Private credit had dried up. Investors were not standing in line to buy a failed hotel.

Today, the city is holding its own on its hotel investment with the expectation that one day a private company will buy the property. Not in dispute is the fact that the entire event center complex—convention center, arena and hotel—has provided a shot in the arm for the downtown.

Nearby, a new CRST Inc. office tower has gone up, and Cedar Rapids-based United Fire Group is moving ahead with plans to add a new office tower to its downtown corporate presence. Another tower, with offices, hotel rooms and apartments, is on the drawing board.

The city's hotel purchase follows other tough choices made by Cedar Rapids City Council members in recent years, which have turned eyesores into community gains.

Former Mayor Lee Clancey, who held office from 1996

through 2001, led the effort to get two closed plants, Iowa Steel and Iowa Iron Works, into the city's hands and torn down. The move laid the foundation for today's flourishing New Bohemia neighborhood next to downtown.

Then, in January 2007, the City Council spent $2 million and the Hall-Perrine Foundation contributed $2 million more to buy the former Sinclair packinghouse property as a next step in redevelopment of the area. About the same time, the city also bought the closed former Heinz Foods facility nearby.

New buildings have been constructed on both former steel plant sites with the support of my City Council colleagues and me, and we also provided support to transform the Heinz Foods site into the popular NewBo City Market.

The Sinclair plant also is gone, thanks to the Federal Emergency Management Agency, which paid to demolish it after the plant had taken on water in the flood of 2008. Much of the site is now becoming a levee as part of the city's flood protection system.

The city's elected leaders have not always been eager to take on troubled properties.

Back in 2001, for instance, a years-long dispute in Cedar Rapids centered on a proposal for the city to help replace a cramped, dilapidated grocery store that served lower-income neighborhoods at a highly visible spot on busy First Avenue East close to Coe College.

At the time, the Chamber of Commerce supported a new store and told me, as head of the Chamber, to try to find the votes on the City Council to get the store built. We saw it as a sensible commitment to older city neighbor-hoods and to the idea that a measured dose of public sup-port can make the difference between blight and progress.

In 2001, council members finally mustered a majority to approve a property-tax incentive for the project, which the Hy-Vee company used to demolish what was there and to build a specially designed, neighborhood grocery store.

Every time I stop in the new store or drive by it, I'm reminded of what an improvement it has made and at the same time how difficult a decision it was back then—to use a city incentive to help a retailer remove a neighborhood blight. But it gave a boost to the store's neighbors, to their property values and to the city's overall property-tax base. I'm convinced that the neighborhoods the store serves are stronger today because of it. Without the effort, they would have continued to decline.

The beleaguered Westdale Mall on Cedar Rapids' west side presented my council colleagues and me with the same issues as the neighborhood Hy-Vee store, only on a larger scale. The mall, which opened in late 1979, began to decline after the larger Coral Ridge Mall opened in 1998 about 20 miles away in Coralville.

By 2007, about half the retail space in Westdale Mall was empty and two of the four anchor stores were gone. That year, the city hired a consultant to help plan a different future for the retail site. But the effort failed to attract a developer.

The mall continued its slide, and residents clamored to know when the city was going to do something about it. My City Council colleagues and I decided to step in.

At the end of 2012, with the help of a city tax-incentive package, local commercial Realtor Scott Byers and developer John Frew, who had managed the work on the city's hotel, convention center and arena projects, joined forces on a new $90 million Westdale redevelopment project. Since then, most of the mall has been demolished, and remaining anchor tenants Younkers and J.C. Penney continue to operate while new buildings, including a hotel, go up around them.

Westdale had been transferred from one real estate entity to another without any new owner willing to put money into it. The property's value had plummeted from $29.7 million to $4.5 million over 12 years with a corresponding drop in revenue from property taxes. The city had been losing by not doing anything.

So how long can a city put up with a failing shopping mall? Or a broken-down neighborhood grocery store, a bankrupt downtown hotel and shuttered industrial plants?

Properties like that turn into symbols of failure. They become inexhaustible fuel for complaints that city officials don't do anything.

Elected officials, though, aren't helpless. We can do more than say "no." We can support private investment, and by doing so, help replace the old and tired, the obsolete, the failed and the unsightly, with something new and better.

28

A GAMBLE FOR DISASTER RECOVERY

I never figured I would be a pitchman for a casino. But I never imagined, either, that I'd be leading a city through recovery from the worst natural disaster in Iowa's history.

Back in the day, I had worked the betting windows at the horse and dog tracks in Nebraska and South Dakota when I attended Morningside College nearby in Sioux City.

But that meant I was a fan of a part-time paycheck to cover college bills, not a fan of gambling.

Even so, my college friend, Jim Sjoerdsma, and I decided in our early twenties to take a chance and invest a little money in a thoroughbred partnership that raced horses in Florida and on the East Coast. All we got out of it that year—1983—were a few photos of horses in the winner's circle that we apparently had some stake in.

The next year, 1984, state-licensed gambling came to Iowa in limited form when the newly created Iowa Racing and Gaming Commission issued a thoroughbred racing license in central Iowa and dog-racing licenses in Dubuque and Waterloo.

Two years later, at age 26, I won my first election to the Iowa House of Representatives. My campaign made no mention of gambling.

By my third year in state office, in 1989, the Legislature and the governor agreed to expand gambling to riverboat casinos, and by fall of that year, voters in eight counties—Dubuque, Lee, Des Moines, Scott, Muscatine, Clinton, Jackson and Woodbury—had approved a referendum to allow riverboat casinos.

Backers of the riverboats sold it as a Mark Twain type of tourist attraction unique to Iowa. But they didn't sell me. I voted no.

In fact, I consistently voted against legislation that established or expanded gambling during my 13 years in the Iowa House. My focus was on supporting the agricultural, manufacturing, insurance and technology industries in Iowa, not the gambling industry.

After I resigned from the Legislature in 1999 to head the Cedar Rapids Area Chamber of Commerce, I looked on in 2003 as local citizens collected thousands of signatures on petitions to bring the issue of casino gambling to a vote in Cedar Rapids and Linn County. I didn't back the idea, nor did the Chamber, and I voted with the majority to turn the gambling measure down.

There was a sense then that Cedar Rapids' shot at a casino had ended.

A Cedar Rapids casino seemed even less likely the next year when the Iowa Racing and Gaming Commission, which had imposed a moratorium on new casinos in 1998, lifted its ban. This led to new casinos opening relatively close to Cedar Rapids—in Washington County to the south in 2006 and in Black Hawk County to the north in 2007.

Not surprisingly, Cedar Rapids gamblers became part of the customer base of the new casinos, something those casinos weren't apt to give up without a fight.

This didn't matter at first. No one had talked publicly about a casino in Cedar Rapids again until the city's crippling flood in June 2008.

Suddenly, there were a lot of moving pieces, each affecting others.

Those included the City Council's decision to build a new convention center, with the help of large federal disaster grant; to renovate the city arena next door; and to buy and renovate the hotel attached to the arena.

Downtowns matter to up-and-coming cities, and we wanted our investment in this event complex—convention center, arena and hotel—to signal to the private sector that Cedar Rapids hadn't thrown in the towel on its flood-damaged downtown.

Our message got through. A group of Cedar Rapids investors stepped forward and asked the city to support the construction of a $150 million-plus casino on mostly city-owned land directly across the Cedar River from downtown.

The plan had one big plus: The proposed Cedar Crossing Casino did not include its own hotel or large entertainment venue. Instead, the investors would depend on the city's hotel, arena and convention center just a few blocks away.

In other words, the city-owned event complex and the proposed casino would work together to help each other succeed.

There were other pluses. The casino had the financial support of hundreds of local investors. In addition, in March 2013, 61.2 percent of voters in our county, Linn, supported a casino in a state-required referendum.

It also was hard to ignore the fact that the casino project

would give a much-needed boost to the Cedar Rapids economy. A casino would mean construction jobs for local workers and companies and local jobs for casino workers. In addition, the casino and an adjoining parking ramp were designed to become a two-block section of the city's future flood protection system.

Advocates for the casino made this point, too: Why should Cedar Rapids and Linn County gamblers, who live in the state's second- largest metropolitan area and second-largest county, be forced to take their local gambling dollars to casinos two or more counties away?

Just as important, the casino would generate property-tax revenue and sales-tax revenue for the city as well as contributions to local non-profit groups.

The revenue from sales tax was a newly important resource for Cedar Rapids for two reasons: potholes and flood protection.

By the end of 2013, Cedar Rapids voters had put in place a 1-percent local-option sales tax to fix streets. Then a month later, the new Iowa Flood Mitigation Board awarded the city more than $260 million for flood protection, which was to be funded over 20 years by a portion of the growth in state sales tax collected in Cedar Rapids.

Suddenly, Cedar Rapids needed to promote taxable sales more than ever—at a casino, hotel, convention center, arena, rejuvenated downtown and elsewhere in the city. A casino would help pull more people into the city to use and enjoy what the city had to offer. And to pay sales tax here, too.

I wasn't kidding myself, though.

I knew that obtaining a state gaming license from the

five-member Iowa Racing and Gaming Commission would not be simple. Previous studies paid for by the commission concluded that casino gambling had saturated much of the state. More significantly, a recent commission study said that a Cedar Rapids casino could take away customers and harm existing casinos, particularly the Riverside Casino & Golf Resort about 40 miles away.

For that reason, the Cedar Rapids investor group, led by Steve Gray, had designed and promoted the proposed Cedar Rapids casino as an urban, downtown casino to set it apart from some of the recently built casinos in more rural parts of the states. I call those, like Riverside, "cornfield" casinos.

Studies paid for by the investors disagreed with the gaming commission's studies and concluded that the casino in Cedar Rapids would add to total state gaming revenue without harming nearby casinos.

In early April 2014, four of the five Racing and Gaming Commission members came to Cedar Rapids to tour the city and the proposed casino site and to hear comments at a public hearing.

I was at the microphone in the front of the bus during a tour of the city's flood-damaged neighborhoods and the casino site, which by then largely had been cleared of flood-ruined commercial properties.

As the commissioners looked out the bus windows, I emphasized that the $150 million-plus casino project was expected to promote another half-billion dollars in private-sector investment in the neighborhood around the casino.

"This is where the opportunity lies," I told the commissioners on the bus. "This is where you as commissioners not only can approve a gaming license and support the gaming industry. This is where you can have your biggest impact on a community in Iowa.

"Because we lost so many homes and businesses, I might be so bold to say, I don't think there is a license that the commission could grant or has granted that could have more economic development impact than a license in Cedar Rapids."

Two weeks later, on a 4-1 vote, the commission denied a state license to the Cedar Rapids project. A Cedar Rapids casino would "cannibalize" customers from the Riverside casino and harm it, the commission majority concluded.

I think the commission made a mistake and focused too narrowly in reaching its decision. It chose to protect an established casino operator rather than back the Cedar Rapids project, a move that I was convinced would have given the overall state gaming industry a shot in the arm, not to mention provide some help to Iowa's second-largest city as it was trying to get back on its feet.

A few months later, in July, the commission granted a gambling license for another rural casino, in Greene County west of Ames, making it the state's 20th state-licensed casino or racetrack. The commission then said it wanted to take a three-year pause before reviewing any new license requests.

I didn't think we needed to stand around in Cedar Rapids like a bunch of stooges.

I turned my attention to the Iowa Legislature and devised a gaming reform proposal that would allow a casino in Cedar Rapids as the state's first smoke-free casino. I was more than willing to have Cedar Rapids be a test case in a state where the casinos have resisted attempts to ban smoking. My idea was that the casino innovation would attract new customers who had not gone to a casino before because of the smoke.

The smoke-free idea generated some legislative committee discussion, but it hasn't come to anything.

Three years pass quickly. As 2017 is starting, the end of the Iowa Racing and Gaming Commission's three-year pause on new casino requests is within sight. The end has not gone unnoticed.

Wild Rose Entertainment, which operates casinos in Clinton, Emmetsburg and Greene County, now is proposing a scaled-back "boutique" casino on a site in downtown Cedar Rapids across from the city's hotel, convention center and arena.

The Cedar Rapids casino investor group, which was denied a state gaming license in 2014 for its proposed Cedar Crossing Casino, also has come forward with its own smaller casino proposal. In the plan, the group would demolish an older city parking ramp and build a casino on the site with parking underneath. The casino would connect directly to the city's hotel, arena and convention center.

This new plan will be presented to the state commission along with the group's original urban destination casino.

I'm not optimistic about any proposal.

Still fresh in my mind is a trip to the Iowa Legislature in the early part of the 2015 legislative session. I appeared with a small delegation from Cedar Rapids in a Senate conference room to make the case for the smoke-free casino concept in Cedar Rapids. The room was packed with Iowa casino industry representatives and lobbyists, and most of the session was taken up by a lesson on the history of gaming in Iowa. There was little time for much consideration of our new idea or any other modification in the state's gaming law.

They gave us a courtesy hearing, and that was it.

Two years later, it's not clear that anything has changed to give proponents hope that they might see casino gaming in Cedar Rapids any time soon.

The composition of the gaming commission is the same, the commission administrator is the same and the Iowa Legislature has not altered the language in the state gaming law to offer additional direction to the commission.

I keep thinking this: The Iowa Legislature created the state gaming industry, but the creation now controls the creator.

29

TWO LEGS SHORT

I'd challenge anyone to try building a $525 million-plus, three-legged stool when one leg is made of federal money, one of state money and one of city money.

By the start of 2017, I had been trying to do it as Cedar Rapids' mayor for seven years.

For now, the stool—a flood protection system for Cedar Rapids—is leaning on one leg.

It is a sturdy single leg, though, thanks to Iowa legislators and Gov. Terry Branstad. In 2012, they created the Iowa Flood Mitigation Board to make financial grants to communities to help them pay for flood protection.

The money for the grants is coming from an idea I proposed that allows communities hit by disaster to use part of the growth in state sales tax collected in the community to help protect against a next disaster.

To date, the state board has awarded grants to 10 Iowa communities totaling more than one-half billion dollars over 20 years to help them build flood protection.

The board's award to Cedar Rapids in December 2013, which has grown to $269.4 million, is large enough that Cedar Rapids is certain it can put a protection system in place over time with the help of city dollars, most yet to be identified. The city's hope for federal funds continues.

For a moment back in 2011, finding all the money that Cedar Rapids would need to build a flood protection system seemed within grasp.

That year, the U.S. Army Corps of Engineers approved a final plan to help build a Cedar Rapids flood protection system, a plan that Congress subsequently authorized.

Quickly, though, we were reminded that authorization of a project is just one of the important "A" words when it comes to federal funding. Another is appropriation—actually having Congress and the president approve the funding.

We had to pick ourselves up from that realization and keep moving.

It was in 2011, too, when Cedar Rapids' prospects first looked good for state funds as the Iowa Legislature took up Cedar Rapids' proposal to allow sharing of sales-tax revenue to help fund flood protection.

However, legislative approval was waiting to see if Cedar Rapids voters were willing to extend the city's existing local-option sales tax to help pay the city's share of the flood protection project.

In the campaign leading up to the local vote, I was the public face for the Protect Cedar Rapids Committee that supported the measure because I had been leading the city's effort to secure federal and state funds for the project.

On the evening of May 3, 2011, committee members, several of my City Council colleagues and I gathered to watch the results of the local tax vote. I can still see our blank faces staring at the TV screen. The tax measure—

which also called for some revenue to be used to fix streets and to lower property taxes—was defeated by 221 votes out of nearly 32,000 votes cast.

I don't know exactly what went wrong. The tax extension was for 20 years and funded more than one community need. Maybe it was for too many years. Some revenue from the existing local-option sales tax, already in place for 63 months to help with flood recovery, had yet to be spent. Maybe that cost votes.

"It was so close and it was so key and so much about our future rests on this," my council colleague Monica Vernon said after the vote count was completed. "It's extremely disappointing. Could we have been clearer? Could we have been simpler?"

Council member Don Karr shook off defeat. "I'll get up and get to work and do something else. Because we've got to have flood protection," he said.

I had planned to head to Des Moines the next morning to report to state lawmakers that local voters had approved the sales-tax extension—and so had done their part to help pay for the city's future flood protection system. But local voters hadn't approved it.

The Iowa Legislature set the state-funding legislation aside.

We had to pick ourselves up again.

Looking back to January 2010, I'll concede that flood protection wasn't the immediate issue on my mind when I took office as Cedar Rapids mayor.

I had campaigned in 2009 promising to quicken the pace of the city's recovery from its 2008 flood. And I think my City Council colleagues and I were doing that.

Even so, my first end-of-winter snowmelt as mayor and the expected spring rains were staring me straight in the face, punctuating for me what life after the 2008 flood would require.

I was reminded that it wasn't enough to recover from the flood. The city also had to find money to build a flood control system to protect against the next one. All the while, too, we had to hope that the next disaster wouldn't come quickly before a protection system was in place.

So that spring of 2010, I started focusing on what I called a three-legged stool of flood protection. We would need federal, state and city money for those three legs—and we didn't have any of it.

To their significant credit, Cedar Rapids City Council members and city officials had invested long hours with expert help at no small cost to outline a flood protection plan for the city in the first months after the June 2008 flood—before I was mayor.

The outline did what it was designed to do. It allowed the U.S. Army Corps of Engineers to use the city's work to speed along the Corps' own plan, which federal rules require before Congress can authorize and fund a project.

In September 2010, the Corps presented its draft plan at public forums in Cedar Rapids. It was no-frills. And much less than we had hoped for.

Federal rules dictate that the Corps must follow a strict benefit-cost ratio, which does not allow it to propose a flood control system that costs more than the value of the property the system protects.

In the Corps' analysis, most of the property value to be protected in Cedar Rapids sits on the east side of the Cedar River—which includes the Quaker Oats Co. plant just north of downtown, the Cargill Inc. corn-processing plant south of downtown, and the downtown itself.

Across the river, older homes made up much of the property, and residential property has a lower value than industrial or commercial property. In addition, much of the west-side property at greatest risk of flooding was being bought out and demolished and did not need a flood control system to protect it.

The Corps concluded that it could support a system that would protect the east side of the river, but could do nothing for the west side.

Well, there was no way we were going to leave the west side of the city unprotected. My City Council colleagues and I didn't think twice. We promised we would protect both sides of the river, though it was unclear where the money to do so would come from.

We also faced reality. We got behind the Corps' plan to partially fund our project, realizing that some federal money, if it ever is appropriated, is better than none.

Then we got busy trying to find more money.

The same month in 2010 that the Corps told us about its one-side-of-the river-plan, a dinner marked the start of Cedar Rapids' ultimately successful effort to obtain state support for flood protection.

I was with City Manager Jeff Pomeranz that evening when I drew out on a restaurant napkin the sales tax-sharing strategy that the Iowa Legislature eventually approved in 2012. Pomeranz still has the napkin.

My idea borrowed from one put together in 2005 by the city of Newton, my Iowa hometown, which had fallen on hard times after its major employer, Maytag, announced that it would close its plant. Cedar Rapids' situation in 2010 wasn't so different. In our case, we were getting back up after a disastrous flood.

My version of the idea would allow Iowa communities hit by a natural disaster to use a portion of the growth in the 6-cent state sales tax collected in a community to fund protection against a future disaster. Newton's plan allowed it to keep state sales-tax revenue generated at the Iowa Speedway to help pay for the racetrack, which opened in 2006 as an economic development attraction for Newton and the state.

Targeted use of state sales tax, which had helped the speedway in Newton, would lead to the creation of the Iowa Flood Mitigation Board in 2012.

So by the start of 2017, Cedar Rapids had some answers about funding its three-legged stool of flood protection.

Its effort at the Iowa Legislature had worked, and the city had secured state funds.

On the federal level, the city's flood project is listed as a priority federal project, but it still must be funded.

The city's share of the project cost will come, most likely, from general city tax dollars over time.

And the protection system on both sides of the Cedar River is being built.

The city's outdoor riverfront amphitheater, which opened in 2013 and rises some 30 feet from the west bank of the Cedar River, doubles as a section of the city's flood protection system. CRST Inc.'s new 11-story downtown office building, which opened in September 2016 across the river from the amphitheater, features a section of flood wall directly in front of it. Levee construction to protect the New Bohemia district and Czech Village below downtown also has begun.

In other words, flood protection will come piece by piece, phase by phase.

In late September 2016, Cedar Rapids had a scare and a chance to wonder anew if it will take a second disaster to remind people of the need for flood protection.

Many days of end-of-summer rains north of Cedar Rapids sent the Cedar River rising to what the National Weather Service was predicting would be historic heights once again in Cedar Rapids, just eight years after its flood disaster of 2008.

With an around-the-clock effort, city workers and contractors hurriedly erected a multimillion-dollar emergency flood protection system in a few days, which held the flooding river back. The water reached 21.95 feet on Sept. 27—the second-highest level on record.

We survived. This time.

I spent much of the last half of 2016 trying to decide whether to seek a third, four-year term as Cedar Rapids mayor in 2017.

Winning a third term would give me a chance to see the city make further strides in building its flood protection system. But the system may need 10, 15 or 20 years before it is completed, so someone else will need to help finish it.

There's always work left to do. Otherwise, a person would stay in the same role forever.

On Dec. 19, I announced at City Hall that I would not seek a third mayoral term.

Over seven years, I've worked with my City Council colleagues, the city's professional staff, community leaders and state and federal officials to help the city recover from one flood disaster and avert a second one while starting construction of a flood protection system.

I'll have one more year in the mayor's office, and I intend to make the most of it.

On March 1, I testified in front of the U.S. Senate Committee on Environment and Public Works, of which Iowa's Sen. Joni Ernst is a member, to once again make the city's case for federal funding to help build Cedar Rapids' flood protection system. Iowa's Sen. Chuck Grassley sat in to listen to my comments.

Afterward, Grassley said it was important for committee members to hear directly from Cedar Rapids' mayor. That way they could better understand the needs of the city, which only barely averted a destructive flood in September 2016 with the city's 2008 flood disaster still fresh in mind.

"The Corps (of Engineers) has to be persuaded to see the common sense of working on prevention and getting the most bang for the buck in the budget," Grassley said. "It just makes sense that we spend millions of dollars now, instead of billions over time to protect life, property and the economic vitality of Cedar Rapids."

This was my sixth or seventh trip to Washington, D.C., since the start of 2010 to talk to federal officials and Iowa's congressional delegation about Cedar Rapids flood recovery and flood protection. Richard Bender, longtime legislative assistant to Iowa's retired Sen. Tom Harkin, often reminded me on these trips that Washington works in decades, not years.

How prophetic. We're coming up on nine years since the city's June 2008 flood.

The one hope hasn't changed: that the Cedar River behaves until the city's flood protection project is fully funded, with federal and city dollars to go along with state dollars, and put in place.

30

COMPLACENCY CAN HURT

Flood survivor Linda Seger gave me the proud owner's tour of her home back in 2009 as I was campaigning to be mayor of Cedar Rapids.

It was the type of expedition that can come only with someone who has rebuilt a ruined house from the studs up after a disaster like the one Cedar Rapids endured in 2008.

Along the way, Seger pointed out how high the floodwater had climbed—as if the water were still as visible as the decorations now back on the living room walls.

We settled into her new kitchen, and a glow came over her.

The kitchen, she said, was so much bigger and more functional than the old box kitchen the house had before the flood.

The kitchen was her favorite place in the house now. She said she just loved it.

I asked why she had not rebuilt it the way it had been, and she said she had a chance to make it better and did.

From this kitchen, Seger emerged to become a leading voice for flood recovery and neighborhood revitalization in the city.

From it, too, I carried with me a sense of what Cedar Rapids' flood recovery might look like and what the city might become.

Cedar Rapids did what Seger did. We set out to build the city better than it had been. We respected what had gotten us here, but we were building for the future.

I think we did what we had promised. That's why, in 2014, the National Civic League named Cedar Rapids an All-America City for the first time in the city's history. It's not just another award. It is a highly prized one given to an elite group of cities that achieve uncommon results in the face of enormous challenges.

The lessons I've learned from Cedar Rapids' rebuilding I now am taking across Iowa.

Since mid-2015, as the founder of think tank Engage Iowa, I've talked to groups in more than 60 of Iowa's 99 counties about improving Iowa's water quality, making Iowa's income-tax system simpler and more competitive and exploring how we can return Iowa's education system to the top among states nationwide.

In the months ahead, I'll be talking, too, about creating jobs, boosting the state's manufacturing sector, bolstering its entrepreneurial business culture and confronting problems of addiction.

On one of my trips in July 2016, business and community leaders welcomed me to Sioux Center in northwest Iowa to hear my thoughts on water quality and taxes. They were friendly and attentive, but as I finished, Larry Den Herder, chairman of the Interstates Companies, asked if I would talk about the "elephant" in the room.

I took off my Engage Iowa hat and said I was aware of speculation that I might run in the 2018 gubernatorial election if Gov. Terry Branstad retired or moved on.

I told the group it was too early to know if I'd run.

I do think that the last two gubernatorial elections in Iowa did not spotlight the big issues facing the state. Branstad defeated incumbent Chet Culver in 2010 in a campaign that focused on the state's budget. And in 2014, Branstad beat Jack Hatch in a race in which Branstad was considered a big front-runner throughout the campaign.

By my reckoning, Iowa hasn't had a robust discussion of issues for nearly a decade. And without a vigorous competition for political office, healthy debates don't happen.

With the start of 2017, talk about the 2018 gubernatorial election has picked up now that Branstad has been picked to be the U.S. ambassador to China and as Lt. Gov. Kim Reynolds gets ready to take his place as governor.

People tell me it would be an uphill battle to run against someone in my own political party who is already in the governor's office. But what worth doing isn't an uphill climb?

I defeated an incumbent in 1986 as a 26-year-old to take a seat in the Iowa House of Representatives. My Republican colleagues in the House picked me as House speaker in late 1994 when I challenged the incumbent speaker. I defeated an incumbent City Council member to become Cedar Rapids mayor. None of that was simple.

I never took on incumbents to challenge them personally. I just had ideas I cared about. I wanted to get things done.

These trips across the state with Engage Iowa have taken me to big cities, the suburbs, small towns and the rural back roads. And in truth, there has been a time or two when uncertainty was riding in the car with me and my friend and associate Andy Anderson as we made our way from one place to another.

You need mental discipline, I've told myself and Andy. You need faith, too.

In one of those head-scratching moments in the summer of 2016, I was to speak to the Rotary Club at its noon luncheon at The Peppertree restaurant on the north edge of Oskaloosa.

Andy and I pulled in about 11:50 a.m. to a parking lot that was all but empty. We climbed out and looked around and at each other. It was hot. We stood there for a minute and kicked the tires—and then shifted into gear. We loaded up a couple of boxes of Engage Iowa material and headed to the door.

"Isn't this fun?" I asked Andy. He assured me it was.

The Rotarians—I'm one—were hyper-punctual. They descended on the place, and by 12:30 p.m., lunch was over and I was talking to a well-fed group of about 30.

It's hard not to believe in Iowans. They always seem willing to get there and give you a chance.

With the new year, I'm seeing a little of my own life in the title of an old Bob Seger song from the 1970s, "Turn the Page."

I've announced I will not seek re-election as Cedar Rapids mayor, I'm on the road more and more with Engage Iowa and I'm weighing the idea of running for governor.

I'm turning the page in my personal life, too. I'm now engaged to marry Carrie Kennedy of Cedar Rapids later in 2017—a life change that will expand the size of my family and circle of loved ones with my five children, her two children, all her relatives and mine, all her friends and my friends, and her cat.

My former wife, Bénédicte, and I continue to be friends and continue to support and cherish our five children.

At this turning point, I'm especially glad that I decided to leave the Iowa Legislature in 1999 when my kids were ages 2 through 7 and my youngest was to come into the world four months later.

Gov. Tom Vilsack was right back then when he said of my Statehouse departure that you can always run for political office again, "but you can only watch your children grow up once."

Today, the kids are great, making their way in the world. Jeremy, 25, is teaching in South Korea and headed to graduate school. After a time at Drake University and in the active-duty Navy, Matthieu, 23, is in his second year at the U.S. Naval Academy. Nicolas, 21, is a senior at Iowa State University and has been accepted to law school. Ana, 19, is a sophomore at Iowa State. And Thomas, 17, a junior at Washington High School in Cedar Rapids, wants to join his brother at the Naval Academy.

So the promise of 2017 has me looking ahead with great expectation.

But it also takes me back to a snowstorm in December 2013 that kept Mike Golic of ESPN's "Mike & Mike" radio show marooned at The Eastern Iowa Airport in Cedar Rapids. The next morning, his co-host, Mike Greenberg, asked listeners for suggestions of what Golic could do in Cedar Rapids.

Suddenly, I received a text message from a friend in Colorado, who was listening to the show and to a Cedar Rapids resident who called in to trash the city. In so doing, the caller tossed in the old criticism of Cedar Rapids as the "City of Five Smells."

The hog plant next to downtown, which was the source of many of the bad odors, had been closed for 20 years, as are the landfill, a former sewage treatment plant and a coal utility plant, all near downtown.

No longer was mention of smells an accurate portrayal of Cedar Rapids. And I felt too good about all the city had accomplished since the flood of 2008 to not want to set the record straight.

Two months later at my annual State of the City Address, I issued a city proclamation that said Cedar Rapids no longer would be the City of Five Smells—if it ever had been. And I called on residents to think of Cedar Rapids in the right way, and to imagine how we could continue to make it better.

As I think about the radio show, I've been wondering if one day soon someone will accuse me of being the critic on the radio because I'm traveling Iowa to talk about ways to improve it.

Listen, I don't want to be the guy who doesn't love Iowa.

I wouldn't be out on the stump if I didn't love the state.

I do think this, though: Sometimes complacency can be the enemy. Sometimes the same isn't enough.

I've read two recent reports about Iowa that conclude the state will gain some jobs and population, but states around Iowa are expected to see greater growth.

It made me wonder: Is Iowa doing all it can to keep pace?

The same is true with education in Iowa, which no longer ranks at the top among states as it once did. And I'm not sure we, as Iowans, have paid much attention to that or have asked why.

I want to be someone who asks.

So I'm committed to being out there, asking questions and talking about the issues. I haven't needed a gubernatorial race to do that, and I don't need one now.

I must say that I haven't seen many others out on the road, and I don't expect I will.

Most days, they don't know what they're missing.

ACKNOWLEDGMENTS

I want to thank Rick Smith for talking to me over many months and for listening and helping put my thoughts and actions into words. Jodi Smith has been the book's content editor, and Deb Schense has handled publication as an editor at her company, Big Fox Publishing, North Liberty, Iowa. The cover design is by Molly Cook of MACook Design, Cedar Rapids.

Financial support for the book did not come from public funds. The book was paid for by the Corbett for Mayor Committee.

I first began contemplating this book in early 2016, halfway through my second term as Cedar Rapids mayor. The support of contributors to my mayoral committee has allowed me to think about what led up to my decision to run for mayor, what I have accomplished and haven't in the job, and how the city was and is now that I've been in office more than seven years.

Many of the contributors went through the Cedar Rapids flood in 2008 in one way or another, and I hope this book highlights some of what came after that disaster.

NOTES

The book features quotes from state and city elected officials and others taken from newspaper stories in The Gazette of Cedar Rapids and The Des Moines Register at the time the comments were made.

Other sources of information are:

Chapter 1

Data on the damage from Cedar Rapids' 2008 flood and the rebuilding after it: city of Cedar Rapids.

Chapter 2

Data on grants from the Iowa Flood Mitigation Board: Iowa Homeland Security & Emergency Management.

Data on grants from the Iowa Community Attraction and Tourism grant program: Iowa Tourism Office, Iowa Economic Development Authority.

Chapter 3

Estimates on grain coming to agricultural-processing plants in Cedar Rapids: Cedar Rapids Metro Economic Alliance.

Number of acres of farmland owned by the city of Cedar Rapids around the city's Eastern Iowa Airport: city of Cedar Rapids.

Chapter 7

Morningside College football records: Morningside College.

Cornell College football records: Cornell College.

Chapter 9

Election results: Linn County Auditor.

Chapter 10

Election results: Linn County Auditor.

Chapter 13

Election results: Linn County Auditor.

Legislative makeup: Iowa Legislature.

Chapter 14

Estimates of damage from 1993 floods in Iowa: "Iowa's Flood Disaster Report."

Chapter 15

Makeup of Congress: U.S. Congress records.

Makeup of the Iowa Legislature: Iowa Legislature.

State election results: Iowa Secretary of State.

Chapter 16

Top tax rates in states, 2016: Tax Foundation.

Chapter 18

Legislative makeup: Iowa Legislature.

Chapter 19

Statewide vote totals: Iowa Secretary of State.

Chapter 20

Information on the size of the Cedar Rapids Area Chamber of Commerce in 1999: Cedar Rapids Metro Economic Alliance.

Data on the state Community Attraction and Tourism grant program and Vision Iowa program: Iowa Tourism Office, Iowa Economic Development Authority.

Election results: Linn County Auditor.

Chapter 21

Information on the Grant Wood-designed window at Cedar Rapids' Veterans Memorial Building: Cedar Rapids Veterans Memorial Commission.

Vote results: Linn County Auditor.

Chapter 22

Data from Cedar Rapids' 2008 flood: city of Cedar Rapids.

The campaign spending in the 2001 Cedar Rapids mayoral race comes from a Gazette news report based on spending reports filed by incumbent Mayor Lee Clancey and challenger and victor, Paul Pate, with the Iowa Ethics & Campaign Disclosure Board.

Election results: Linn County Auditor.

Chapter 23

Buyout data provided by officials from Waterloo and Iowa City in news accounts at the time.

Chapter 24

Data on unchanging city property tax levy: city of Cedar Rapids.

Statewide data on local-option sales taxes in place across Iowa: Iowa Department of Revenue.

Chapter 25

The list of Cedar Rapids building projects receiving state I-JOBS grants: city of Cedar Rapids.

Statewide election results: Iowa Secretary of State.

Chapter 27

Cost figures for hotel purchase and renovation: city of Cedar Rapids.

Changing property valuation of Westdale Mall property: Cedar Rapids City Assessor.

Chapter 28

History of the gaming industry in Iowa: Iowa Racing and Gaming Commission.

Election results: Linn County Auditor.

Chapter 29

Cost estimate of $525 million for the Cedar Rapids flood protection system is in 2017 dollars: city of Cedar Rapids.

Data on state grants for flood protection to 10 Iowa communities: Iowa Flood Mitigation Board.

PHOTO CREDITS

Front Cover: Crystal LoGiudice, The Gazette.

Back Cover: Ed Kempf, Impact Photography / Joe Photo, Cedar Rapids.

Pages 1–3: Corbett family photos.

Pages 4–5: John McIvor, The Gazette.

Page 6: Top: Paul Jensen, The Gazette. Others: Ron Corbett photos.

Page 7: Ron Corbett photo.

Page 8: Photos from The Gazette.

Page 9: Top: Cliff Jette, The Gazette. Bottom: Jim Slosiarek, The Gazette.

Page 10: Top: Jonathan Woods, The Gazette. Bottom: Greg Henshall, the Federal Emergency Management Agency.

Page 11: Top: Jim Slosiarek, The Gazette. Bottom: Brian Ray, The Gazette.

Page 12: Top: Brian Ray, The Gazette. Bottom: Liz Martin, The Gazette.

Page 13: Top: Julie Koehn, The Gazette. Bottom: Jim Slosiarek, The Gazette.

Page 14: Top: Adam Wesley, The Gazette. Bottom: Adam Wesley, The Gazette.

Page 15: Top: Liz Martin, The Gazette. Bottom: Justin Wan, The Gazette.

Page 16: Top: Liz Martin, The Gazette. Bottom left: Adam Wesley, The Gazette. Bottom right: Liz Martin, The Gazette.

Page 17: Top: Liz Martin, The Gazette. Bottom left and right: Brian Ray, The Gazette.

Page 18: Liz Martin, The Gazette.

Page 19: Top: Rebecca Miller, The Gazette. Middle: Liz Martin, The Gazette. Bottom: Adam Wesley, The Gazette.

Page 20: Stephen Mally, The Gazette.

ABOUT

Ron Corbett won a seat in the Iowa House of Representatives at age 26. A Republican, he served in the Legislature for 13 years, becoming the youngest House speaker in Iowa history. He left in 1999 to head the Cedar Rapids Area Chamber of Commerce and to be home full time to help raise his five children. He was a community leader and coalition-builder in six years at the Chamber. In 2009, he was elected Cedar Rapids mayor with a pledge to speed up the city's recovery from a flood in 2008—the worst disaster in the state's history. Now in his eighth year as mayor, he has played a key role in the community's comeback. Outside of City Hall, he operates Engage Iowa, a conservative think tank he founded in 2015, as he contemplates a run for governor. A Newton (Iowa) High School graduate, he holds a bachelor's degree in business from Cornell College in Mount Vernon, Iowa.

Rick Smith grew up in western Pennsylvania not far from Ron Corbett's boyhood home. Like Corbett, Smith has spent his adult working life in Iowa. He earned a bachelor's degree in history from the University of Pennsylvania and a master's degree in journalism from the University of Iowa. Smith worked as a news reporter for The Gazette in Cedar Rapids for 32 years before retiring at the end of 2015. He covered local government and local politics for the last half of his Gazette career, including reporting and writing about the city's 2008 flood disaster and recovery.